MON...
GER...
GERMANTOWN, MARYLAND
W9-CIK-944
...RY
...LIBRARY
BCJ 1 0 2012

LATINAS
in the WORKPLACE

AN EMERGING LEADERSHIP FORCE

Esther Elena López-Mulnix,
Mimi Wolverton,
and Salwa A. Zaki

1996–2011 15TH ANNIVERSARY

Sty/us

PUBLISHING, LLC.

STERLING, VIRGINIA

133567824
OCT 10 2012

Sty/us

COPYRIGHT © 2011 BY STYLUS PUBLISHING, LLC.

Published by Stylus Publishing, LLC
22883 Quicksilver Drive
Sterling, Virginia 20166-2102

All rights reserved. No part of this book may be
reprinted or reproduced in any form or by any
electronic, mechanical or other means, now known or
hereafter invented, including photocopying, recording
and information storage and retrieval, without
permission in writing from the publisher.

Library of Congress Cataloging-in-Publication-Data
López-Mulnix, Esther Elena, 1954-
    Latinas in the workplace : an emerging leadership
force / Esther Elena López-Mulnix, Mimi Wolverton
and Salwa A. Zaki.—1st ed.
    p.   cm.
Includes bibliographical references and index.
ISBN 978-1-57922-352-6 (cloth : alk. paper)
ISBN 978-1-57922-353-3 (pbk. : alk. paper)
  1. Hispanic American women in the professions—Case
studies.   2. Leadership in women—United States—
Case studies.   I. Wolverton, Mimi. II. Zaki, Salwa A.,
1965–   III. Title.
HD6057.5.U5L67   2011
331.4089'68073—dc22

                                          2010022575

13-digit ISBN: 978-1-57922-352-6 (cloth)
13-digit ISBN: 978-1-57922-353-3 (paper)

Printed in the United States of America

All first editions printed on acid free paper
that meets the American National Standards Institute
Z39–48 Standard.

Bulk Purchases

Quantity discounts are available for use in
workshops and for staff development.
Call 1-800-232-0223

First Edition, 2011

10 9 8 7 6 5 4 3 2 1

WITHDRAWN

LATINAS
in the WORKPLACE

THE JOURNEYS TO LEADERSHIP SERIES

The *Journeys to Leadership Series* is about successful women who have reached the pinnacle of their careers. It features stories about extraordinary women who have found paths to success—whether it is leading a college or university or becoming successful scholars in science and engineering or thriving in some other male-dominated arena.

Available

Answering the Call
African American Women in Higher Education Leadership
Beverly L. Bower and Mimi Wolverton

Women at the Top
What Women University and College Presidents
Say About Effective Leadership
Mimi Wolverton, Beverly L. Bower, and Adrienne E. Hyle

To the eight courageous Latinas who welcomed the opportunity to share their leadership journeys in order to facilitate those of daughters and granddaughters everywhere.

CONTENTS

Contents

ACKNOWLEDGMENTS

This book has been a labor of love and our own fascinating journey over terrain not often explored—the struggles and successes of Latina leaders. We are indeed indebted to the women featured in this book for taking time out of their busy schedules to share their stories with us. We also thank our families for their ongoing support: Michael William Mulnix for challenging Esther to experience the writing of this book as an opportunity; Dalia and Khalil Zaki for teaching their mom, Salwa, something new each day; and Marv Wolverton, who always provides Mimi with a steady hand and an encouraging word. We are also truly appreciative of our publisher, John von Knorring, for his support of and faith in our endeavor, and of the hardworking staff at Stylus for all their assistance.

Photograph of Sally Garza Fernandez on page 34 was taken by Andrew Stegmeyer.
Photograph of Carmella Franco on page 48 was taken by Laurie Weidner.
Photograph of Breatriz Salcedo-Strumpf on page 110 was taken by Daniel Strumpf.

FOREWORD

Tina Cordova, one of the Latinas featured in this book, calls *Latinas in the Workplace* a "labor of love for our people, of Hispanas." She goes on to say, "Our stories don't always get told like they should. I am so glad the authors chose me to be part of it." If asked, each of the women whose stories we tell in *Latinas in the Workplace* would agree with Cordova's sentiment.

Out of curiosity I ran three quick searches on a popular Internet site of a book retailer. The term *leaders* resulted in over forty-five thousand entries. *Women leaders* brought up almost fifteen hundred listings. *Latina leaders* elicited only thirty responses, ten of which are books devoted exclusively to Latinas, and one of those is out of print. Tina's observation seems understated at best. In writing this book we hope to help rectify the situation.

Latinas in the Workplace features the stories of eight exceptional women. It is the third book in the **Journeys to Leadership** Series. The series features stories about extraordinary women who have found paths to success—whether in higher education, public schools, business, science, or some other male-dominated arena.

The first two books in the series, *Women at the Top* and *Answering the Call*, introduce us to women who are leaders in higher education—college presidents and women who work in the policy arena. *Latinas in the Workplace* moves beyond this sector. This book highlights the stories of a foundation president, two business CEOs, a doctor, a former college president, a teacher and author, and two school superintendents.

We invite you to join us in celebrating these exceptional women, their lives, and their careers. Their stories merit telling and their voices need to be heard. All of us, men and women alike, can learn about leadership from them. They are at the forefront of a leadership movement in the United States. We hope that their stories inspire others—Latinas and women in general—to follow in their footsteps.

Mimi Wolverton, Series Editor
Journeys to Leadership

one

JOURNEYS TO SUCCESS

Esther Elena López-Mulnix

I received the invitation to collaborate on this book more than two years ago. I was thrilled with the opportunity to investigate the successful paths Latinas in the United States are walking. Yet, I was aware of the demands this would impose. On one hand I anticipated an amazing learning journey, but on the other hand it seemed a journey that would necessitate many hours, hours that I did not have at my disposal. I had self-doubts. English is not my first language—could I deliver? I thought about declining the invitation, a similar reaction on my part to challenging opportunities that have presented themselves in the past, opportunities like teaching at my alma mater at a very young age, relocating to the United States, having children, getting my doctorate, becoming an academic in the United States, founding and editing two journals, and now writing a book. Yet, like most people, I want to leave some kind of legacy for the next generation. So I accepted the challenge, and I am glad that I did.

ESTHER ELENA LÓPEZ-MULNIX

I T HAS BEEN AN amazing learning experience. Sarita Brown, Tina Cordova, Sally Garza Fernandez, Carmella Franco,

Christine Johnson, Thelma López-Lira, Darline Robles, and Beatriz Salcedo-Strumpf have generously shared their lives with us in a candid manner giving details of their experiences.

Their journeys begin with the word *success*. Even though the meaning of success for our participants varies, an overarching, almost implicit, understanding exists among them. For the women featured in this book, success means having accumulated enough material wealth to have the freedom to choose where and how to invest time and energy. Brown makes choices about how to focus her career. Cordova enjoys the flexibility to meet the needs of her extended family. Fernandez takes the time to mentor and support her daughter. Johnson and Salcedo-Strumpf nurture their bodies, minds, and souls. All of them seek professional and personal balance and enjoy the luxury of defining that balance.

They create their own success. Yet their journeys are rooted in similar ground tilled long before they entered the work world—a strong sense of family, influential religious traditions, and formidable ties to their cultural heritage.

Our eight women experienced a strong sense of family as children and continue to value family—both immediate and extended—as adults. Salcedo-Strumpf comes from a family of ten. Johnson remains close to her brothers. López-Lira's siblings helped raise her. Franco had twenty-one first cousins, several of whom she counts as dear friends. Today, Fernandez is in partnership with her daughter, and Brown built a family of friends for hers. And Cordova's father, son, brothers, nephew, cousins, and partner have all worked for her company at one time or another.

Many of our contributors developed particularly strong relationships with their fathers or grandmothers. López-Lira speaks of learning much from her *abuela* (grandmother). Robles remembers her grandmother loading her and her cousins into the car along with used clothes, flour, and beans and making repeated trips to relatives in Mexicali. Salcedo-Strumpf and her grandmother had such a strong relationship that her grandmother learned to read and write so she could communicate with her granddaughter when she moved to the United States. Johnson tells us about a letter her father wrote to her on her 10th birthday. She says, "I read it every year on my birthday. It's a treasure."

These Latinas grew up with an extreme determination to get educated that was fostered by parents and grandparents who believed education was the path to success. López-Lira's mother made sure her children succeeded. The first step was college. Fernandez's grandfather insisted she learn English because he believed it was the path to success. All of them have engaged in postgraduate college work and hold advanced degrees. Engrained in each of them is a sense of honor, the need to treat others with respect, and an inner strength, qualities nurtured by family members. Fernandez summarizes her approach to leadership as engaging, one that demonstrates humility and respect for others. Cordova simply says, "My family, the family that raised me, is a significant part of who I am."

For these women, family is an inclusive term. They relate to those around them as though they were family. Johnson "yearned to use [her] time in service to others, to be a blessing to those around [her]." Robles believes firmly that "education should unlock the hidden treasures of sympathy, kindness, and generosity from the soul of a child." Cordova feels her employees and their families are her responsibility. "At a party for employees and their families . . . I was able to see the company all together. I saw the children's faces. It was overwhelming, knowing they all count on me." Fernandez's family "has always given back to [its] community by helping those in need," and she emulates their behavior.

Religion seemed engrained in the family lives of these women as children. In some, religion played a dominant role. Johnson and Cordova are Catholic—"profoundly Catholic" in Johnson's case and "strongly" in Cordova's. Johnson states, "All the fundamentals of me come from my faith." Cordova is a "faith-filled woman." For her, "faith brings with it a kind of peace, reconciliation, and optimism." For others, religion seems a less prominent life factor, yet still an influence. Salcedo-Strumpf was raised Catholic and married a Jewish man and finds the combination broadens her worldview. Brown's father was Catholic, her mother Jewish. She is raising her daughter in the Jewish faith. López-Lira doesn't mention religion per se, but her daughter attends a Catholic high school.

Even when not specifically mentioned, the church appears to have been there, its teachings reinforcing the values instilled by their families. The desire to give back is a fundamental cornerstone of Catholicism and Judaism. And this desire had an impact on the decisions our Latinas made. Brown says, "I'm not a missionary, but what I'm doing now is a life calling. I feel called to improve the status of Latino students." Franco speaks of helping others as a "moral imperative." Robles alludes to the role of religion in guiding her actions. Johnson views her abilities as gifts to be used to uplift humanity.

Family and religion work in concert to create culture. They intertwine to build traditions, language, and belief systems. Cultures define what is valued, and the intersection of cultures, being Mexicana and being American, can negatively and positively affect a society and its members. These Latinas are bicultural and bilingual, qualities that have profoundly shaped who these women are.

In some instances, negative realities spawned positive opportunities. Even though Cordova's family had lived in New Mexico for generations, her father's negative racially motivated experiences made him decide that his children had to be proficient in English; he said, "If you learn Spanish later, that's fine." Brown grew up in New York but as a teenager moved to Texas, where being Mexicana took on new meaning. "Being Mexicana was an insult. We were expected not to succeed." These attitudes helped motivate her to defy expectations.

In others, a subtler inner-cultural conflict engendered the same response. Salcedo-Strumpf asserts, "There is *machismo* everywhere in the world—just different degrees of it. By the time I was in my twenties, I was tired of the machismo in our Mexican society." Likewise, López-Lira holds closely what she calls her "power," her independence. "The worst mistake I made was postponing my own goals. I did not try to fail but I didn't try to succeed either. I waited for my partner to succeed so that I could start investing in myself. I think now this was the wrong tactic." Even years into her career Robles encountered a similar male mentality. When she was offered a job in Utah, one Latino board member believed that because she is Latina, she would never leave her family or community. "It was the first time in a long time where someone actually believed that just because I am Latina I didn't have choices."

No matter what negative experiences they might have had, these women see cultural heritage as a distinct advantage. Salcedo-Strumpf believes "having two cultures gives [her] a unique perspective and two distinct ways of dealing with people." López-Lira adds a touch of realism, "I can't change people's culture. I have to work with it." Her ability to function across cultural lines brings focus to this need. To Franco, "being Latina and [her] ability to speak [her] family language had been assets throughout [her] life. It opened doors." When she became a superintendent "the icing on the cake" was that she could speak

Spanish. Cordova continually reaps rewards: "My first language is English and I am fairly fluent in Spanish, and being bilingual is a real benefit in the business world."

Their backgrounds, experiences, and cultural heritages reflect nuances. Salcedo-Strumpf's husband is Jewish and American, which has given her insight into those cultures as well as her Latino birth culture. Johnson suggests, "My background gives me a unique cultural fingerprint—rural, western, Anglo, Hispanic, and Catholic. The combination provides me with wonderful perspective."

These differences are subtle and to some extent manifest themselves in the language they use to describe who they are as individuals. Cordova's ancestors never moved but have lived in Mexico and the United States—their citizenship subject to shifting national borders. Hence, she is proud of her Hispanic heritage. Brown is a Mexicana. Her parents wrestled with ethnicity (Mexican, Eastern European, and American) and religion (Catholic and Jewish) years ago as they forged a life together in New York. Robles, born and raised in California, has always known that she is a Mexican American but also uses Latina as a more generic catchall term. Franco, who also grew up in California, uses the term *Latina* when she refers to herself.

Today, Latina leaders represent a relatively small percentage of women in leadership in the United States. In fact, Latinas hold less than 1 percent of corporate office and board of director positions in Fortune 500 companies and similarly miniscule percentages in professions like medicine, higher education, and K–12 administration.

The U.S. Bureau of Labor Statistics analyzes the workforce and types of employment using criteria such as earnings and education attainment. One of its primary categories is Management,

Professional, and Related Occupations. For the general population (men and women sixteen years and older), this category is
further segmented into over five hundred subcategories that include occupations such as CEOs and doctors but also farmers
and ranchers, midlevel managers, ministers, legislators, police
and firefighters, accountants and auditors, computer program-
mers, teachers, nurses, physical therapists, scientists and techni-
cians, pilots, secretaries, parking lot attendants, and the like.
When the bureau further examines women in the workforce by
race and ethnicity, it appears there are so few women in some of
these subcategories that it uses only the broadest classifications
to summarize the data. Latinas constitute about 6 percent of the
general work population but make up less than 4 percent of the
Management, Professional, and Related Occupations category.
And there is really no way to tell how many Latinas fill top-level
leadership positions, but an educated guess suggests that the
number is small. Brown comments, "For many people overriding assumptions about who will fulfill leadership roles do not
start with Latinas."

Latinas constitute one of the fastest-growing segments of our
population with 13 percent of the total female population and 21
percent of the under-five-years-old group, all of whom need role
models. The few Latinas in leadership, however, lack visibility.
As Robles put it, "It's not easy to get your hands on information
about Latina success stories to share and talk about with young
women."

Our eight women represent a diverse group of Latinas at the
forefront of a leadership movement in the United States. They
are part of an emerging leadership force that will grow as the
presence of Latinas in the general labor pool increases. We hope
that these women's stories inspire not only their contemporaries
but the next generation of Latinas as well.

BIBLIOGRAPHICAL NOTE

We give special thanks to Aurelia Flores, founder of Powerful Latinas, for providing her insights on Latinas in the workforce. For those interested in a more in-depth look at current statistical information about Latinas in the workforce we suggest the following websites:

http://www.powerfullatinas.com
http://www.catalyst.org
http://www.bls.gov/cps/wlftablell.htm
http://www.bls.gov/cps/wlftable12.htm

AUTHORS' NOTE

In telling their stories, we combine first- and third-person perspectives. The former lets the reader listen directly to these women. We narrate their stories to move them along, but each woman tells her own story in her own words. Each story's final rendering was created from the individual's personal recollections, speeches, institutional websites, and newspaper and journal articles written about her. We omitted in-text references because we believe that they intrude on the story being told. At the end of each chapter we provide a brief bibliographical note that highlights the main resources used in telling that particular story. At the end of the book, we have included a detailed explanation of the research process used to generate these stories.

two

STUDENTS' SUCCESS
IS THE YARDSTICK

Sarita Brown

"I F YOU WERE TO ASK ME to describe myself, I'd use three key words: optimistic, driven, and energetic. It's very simple. I tend to look for the good side of people and events. For example, I am optimistic about today's economic situation. Institutions of higher education are cutting back; people are tightening their belts. It is a sobering and serious time. My optimism lies in the way I address this. I say, 'Yes, the scenario is tough but for this generation of students this is their only moment.' The Hispanic Scholarship Fund is producing very positive opportunities for Latino students right now. It was not easy, but by working with several constituencies, corporate America, college alumni, and the like, and focusing *Excelencia*'s (a not-for-profit organization devoted to Latino success in higher education) energies on public policy and public strategies I helped create this opportunity. I leveraged strategic information. In short, I concentrate on the ideal or the aspiration and then work to make it happen.

"Driven? Well, that's what people say about me. I agree. I am driven. I have tenacity and direction in terms of my work and how I go about life. I have grown very committed to helping people, especially Latino students. I want other individuals who say that they are committed to helping Latino students to move past what I consider the 'lethal comfort level.' People talk about the gap in achievement levels. We're comfortable talking about it; we've been doing so for ten years. We know that there are a lot of Latinos in this country. We know that Latinos are the youngest population and that in the coming decade they will play a significant role in American society. But somehow we feel that just by talking about it, something has happened. To me, those statements are like 'setting the table for dinner. But, where is the food?' I call it lethal because the goal has become the quantification of this phenomenon, not the resolution of its accompanying problems and issues. It's not about chronicling, it's about responding, about taking responsibility, about engaging. When I look at the demographics and disparate achievement levels, I crank up the heat to make 'the chroniclers' uncomfortable. I expect more of myself; I expect better results; and I expect others to do the same. That's my definition of driven.

"And what do I mean by energetic? I have a romantic sense of work. When you get to the top it's like running a marathon. You have to have the energy to perform. I rarely just 'do' a job. I engage in a passion. The job is the setting and the context in which I do my work. Passion gives me the energy I need. I am very lucky to have found a cause that I'm passionate about, work to which I can give my full energy.

"I'm not a missionary, but I see what I do as my life's calling. I feel called to improve the status of Latino students. I'm contributing to a much larger effort, searching for, ensuring, and promoting educational opportunities for today's underserved. In many ways, what I do is more than running a marathon especially if you think of a marathon as a personal race or a singular effort within a larger race. Instead for me, it's about all of us reaching the finish line, of really making a contribution. It's making sure low income and minority students receive every possible opportunity to succeed, so they too can contribute to the greater good.

"My father was born in Chihuahua, Mexico, and his family immigrated to Los Angeles when he was young. I knew about my grandparents on my father's side. But I interacted with them in person only sporadically. Most of the time they were voices over the telephone and cards I received in the mail. I was greatly influenced by my father. He left school when he was in the third grade. He worked hard and he was very smart, street smart. These traits—working hard and being street smart—influenced me. I grew up believing that if I worked really hard and could figure things out, I could walk into any situation, size people up, and make the situation work for me. Even though these traits are not uniquely Mexican, my general view of the Mexican people as I was growing up was of a people who worked hard and could do amazing things if they set their minds to it.

"On my mother's side, I didn't know my grandparents. My grandmother was originally from Bohemia, Czechoslovakia, and her husband, my blood grandfather, died when my mother was a baby. The most significant part of my mother's heritage was her faith. She was Jewish; therefore, I'm also Jewish, because I was born of a Jewish mother. My mother was not terribly well trained in Judaism, but she did her part to make sure that I was introduced to the Jewish tradition. My father was very supportive of that.

"My parents are no longer living but in their time they were really adventurous—real trendsetters. They wrestled with race, ethnicity, and religion years ago as they forged a life together. Now, with the Obama administration, everyone is talking as if intercultural, cross-cultural, interfaith relationships are somehow

new. Not so! My father, who was raised Catholic, was not prepared to tell the priest that his child would be raised Catholic,
just as my mother wouldn't guarantee the rabbi that her daughter
would be Jewish. They ended up getting married by a Methodist
minister. Believe me, the life they made for me was very rich
indeed!

"I was born in New York City. We lived in Washington Heights
in Manhattan. It was a wonderful, happy time. We lived in a two-
room apartment. We walked up five flights of stairs to reach our
floor. My father was a waiter and my mother worked part-time in
temporary jobs while I was in school. I lived with two people who
were enthusiastic about what a city like New York had to offer. I
took classes at the Ninety-Second Street Y. I went to the Museum
of Natural History. My mother and I went to matinees on Sunday
afternoons. I remember seeing *Man of La Mancha* the year we
moved to Texas. Financially, our existence was quite modest, but
my parents were the type of people who said, 'The world is your
oyster, go out and find pearls.' This is the richness I had, a richness of the exposure to multiple cultural experiences.

"During those early days, one of the most distinctive memories I have was knowing I was Mexicana. Being Mexicana in New
York City was like saying you were Brazilian. It provided no
frame of reference (good or bad) for most people including our
Puerto Rican and Cuban neighbors. It carried no negative conno-
tations at all. I just was Mexicana. I didn't experience any sense
of racism or prejudice.

"By the time I was ten, Washington Heights had begun to
change and not in a good way. Drugs came into our neighborhood. It created safety issues. So my father decided we should
move. It could have been anywhere, really. He talked about Philadelphia because he believed that it was a 'safe' city, but we ended
up in Texas. He'd taken a bus trip to Los Angeles to visit his

family and on the way, stopped in San Antonio to visit a guy he knew who had become a very successful businessman and had opened up a fancy restaurant and bar.

"Dad came back from that trip telling my mother and me that we were moving to San Antonio, that he had bought a house! He had asked the real estate agent which school district was the best. He knew if I went to a good enough school the chances of me going to college would be very high. And he was right. Years later I earned two degrees at the University of Texas, a bachelor's in ethnic studies and a master's in communication.

"We moved into a neighborhood where, to this day, the people living there are known as the '09ers' because those are the last two digits of the zip code. It is now a wealthy area with very few Mexican people. It takes my breath away when I think about the courage he had.

"From that point on, however, the meaning of being Mexicana shifted 180 degrees. And while I would have always been my father's daughter and proud to be Mexicana, my whole view would have been radically different had we stayed in New York or moved to Pennsylvania. In Texas, my understanding of being Mexicana changed and this new understanding shaped me profoundly. Being Mexicana in San Antonio was an insult. We were expected not to succeed. The community had very low expectations and little respect for Mexican individuals. It was a radical life's lesson that impacted the direction of my life and my entire life's work.

"I was in the fifth grade when we moved. I remember being in the lunch room the first semester in my new school. I was sitting next to a friend and a boy came up to me and said, 'You are in my seat.' I told him I'd gotten there first and his face got all red and he blurted out, 'You Mexicans!' I was really surprised, not hurt, just surprised. You see, he didn't even know I was Mexican. It was just the worst thing he could think of to call me.

"I am the only child of two only children. I think that one of my responses to being an only child is that I have made a family of friends. Some of them have been my friends for thirty-five or forty years. I love the fact that many of them knew my parents and that they can talk now to my six-year-old daughter, Amara, about them. She is fond of saying, 'I have one of the biggest families ever!'

"Currently, my daughter and I live by ourselves in Virginia. I have constructed a life that is totally enhanced by technology. It allows me to multitask better than I ever thought possible. For example, this morning I made a cup of coffee and was online by six working on a document for a report that needs to be released next week. An hour later, Amara came downstairs. Sometimes we work on homework. Amara is very bright and responsive and has learned a great deal without much conscious effort. Reading is not one of those things. She is still trying to learn how to read. We work hard on it together. No homework this morning. As I made breakfast, a friend called and we discussed the fact that I was not going to an event tonight with the Gates Foundation because I had to finish this report. I took a break from writing and Amara and I walked a block and a half to her public elementary school. One hour later Dr. Jill Biden's chief director of policy e-mailed me about tonight's event. She had seen my colleague— the one I was speaking with on the phone. She has questions she hopes I can answer. And so the day goes. Now, the reason all this works is because I can be online or on the phone, walk my daughter, come back, and never be disconnected. I have a fluid and integrated life that allows me to do everything.

"My office is in downtown Washington, D.C., near DuPont Circle but I work all over the place. In 2004, I co-founded and am now president of a not-for-profit organization called *Excelencia* in Education. Before that I founded the Hispanic Scholarship Fund Institute. It was the first iteration of *Excelencia* and no longer exists. The institute focused on public policy that supported Latino education.

"I've also worked in government at state and national levels. When I was still in Texas, I built a national model at the University of Texas for promoting minority success in graduate education. During the Clinton administration I served as the executive director of the White House Initiative on Educational Excellence for Hispanic Americans, which advised the president on the educational condition of Latino Americans. I spent three years as a political appointee in the Clinton administration, a small part of my life.

"The overarching commitment since the beginning of my career has been to improve educational opportunities and systems so that more students thrive. Early on I centered on issues about Latinos. It just so happens that I did that while I was involved in government. I am not a political person but the experience was consequential. My lifelong calling and my wonderful responsibility in the Clinton administration intersected and led me in a more focused direction.

"I did not work for either Bush administration, but we interface closely with the new [Obama] administration on a number of policy issues. For example, Obama's administration has talked about wanting to increase college degree production among Latino students and, basically, *Excelencia* has been saying since its inception that it is impossible to imagine our country achieving its goals without this happening. Our future economic strength and global competitiveness is predicated on successful human capital. What that means is an educated workforce with at least some level of post-secondary education.

"Ever since the 2000 census, the public, educators, policy makers, and business leaders have speculated about the implications of the profound demographic shift from the baby boomer generation to today's young people of high school and college age, many of whom are Latino. The aim of *Excelencia* in Education is to shape the country's response to this trend by increasing and accelerating Latino student success in higher education. By linking research, policy, and practice, *Excelencia* works to inform policy makers and institutional leaders and to promote policies and practices that support higher educational achievement for these students. If we succeed with Latinos we are effective with all students because what is good for the former also benefits the latter. We focus a great deal of our efforts on Hispanic-Serving Institutions. For instance, *Leading in a Changing America: Presidential Perspectives From Hispanic-Serving Institutions*, a 2009 research report, provides a closer view of effective leadership, institutional practices, and guiding principles that support Latino student success. Regularly we prepare policy briefs at the federal level that deal with immigrant workers, how Latinos fund their education, and who our Latino students are. At the state level, we concentrate on policy issues in the border states of Texas, New Mexico, Arizona, and California. Data drive our research.

"Each day of my life is very different, and that makes it interesting. Most days are filled with half a dozen meetings, either on the phone or in person. At *Excelencia* we're going through a growth spurt right now. We're running two new programs. Through one program, Growing What Works, we offer twenty grants each worth $50,000 to institutions to fund pilot programs designed to further student success. During 2009 we received over 210 applications. We had an internal review committee with three staff members, and an external review committee of six individuals. We were able to make the full assessment and recipient selection in less than six months. It was great, just a whole lot of work. The need for such grants in higher education is huge and twenty is only the beginning.

"Another program, the Accelerating LAtino Student Success (ALASS) Project, involves a confederation of institutions. If we are going to keep talking about the 'changing demographics' in this country then we need a tactical plan to deal with such change. We are at a point where we must look at what is happening to our future workers. Graduation rates for Latinos are flatlining and transfer rates for Latinos from community colleges to upper-degree-granting institutions are very poor. What I say to young people is this: 'Okay, guys. Now is the time!' Student success is the yardstick by which I measure mine. That's the driving philosophy behind the ALASS Project.

"I'm fifty-three this year. I think about the amount of time I've spent on this particular issue [helping Latinos succeed in education] and this calling. I think a lot about my daughter, what I want to do for her, how I want to bring to her attention the things I value most, and how I can create the best opportunities for her. She is young; most of my friends have children who are in their early twenties and thirties. Their children have long since graduated from college. I do have a peer group of other parents who, like me, are older. That combination of friends with both younger and older children keeps it all fresh and interesting. The contrast between these two very different groups provides a rich experience. I know a lot about Dora the Explorer, the wizards in the Harry Potter stories, and Chuck E. Cheese playtime as well as what motivates college students. My mind's perspective is quite broad.

"My life revolves around my daughter, especially on weekends. On Saturdays we do mommy-related activities like play dates and birthday parties. On Sunday mornings while she is in religious school at the Agudas Achim Synagogue in Alexandria, Virginia, I have social time with my friends. I like to entertain. I have an annual Tamales-Latkes Fest. The big feature is food.

"My mother and I had a difficult relationship. Today I realize that by my age most people have gained a certain amount of wisdom, about both the good and the bad. But when I was young I didn't see it. I always felt I had something to prove, especially to my mother. My parents had tough upbringings and she was angry about it. I was the closest person around so I became the target of her frustration. She said that she loved me and she wanted good things for me, but some of her behavior didn't reflect what she said. My father dreamed of a better life for me. I absorbed the power of the juxtaposition of both. These two experiences showed me that in the end it comes down to your response to this question: 'What are you going to do about it?' Bad stuff happens; you can't hide or be foolish and do yourself in. So what do you do about it? My father's love and support gave me the courage to fight for my space. He brought meaning to the statement, 'I want things to be better for my child.' What moves me most about my father is that he loved me and supported me in ways that he never experienced in his own upbringing. He was a resilient man who could imagine what love is even if he hadn't received it.

"Although I would have preferred a different path with my mother, our relationship gave me an appreciation for the difficulty many people have in dealing with family members, and I understand how this shapes their lives. Sometimes such conflict can be harnessed and turned into a drive for success—proof that you are living with a purpose and that you can make good things happen even out of a less than positive experience. I learned that the hard way from my mother. I was tested and found I could depend on myself. I knew I could produce and that I could work hard and succeed. I believe my mother was able to see that before she died. I have tried to establish a more congenial bond with my daughter.

"It seems as if Latinas start at a disadvantage—one level below everyone else. I think that's our culture. Latinas even today have to work really hard to be recognized as leaders, to be included. There is nothing we can take for granted about the full participation of Latinas. I acknowledge that the 'landscape' is biased against Latina women. I know the challenges I face because I am a woman and Latina—the lack of instant rapport, for instance, and the fact that some men are still challenged when working with or for women.

"For many people overriding assumptions about who will fulfill leadership roles do not start with Latinas, and we still have a male-focused assumption about leadership. I am constantly tested, but in some respects the situation is analogous to 'It's cold outside, so put a coat on.' Sometimes when women examine this issue, I feel alienated from the conversations because the comments turn in large part to the negative influence of men. Everyone needs support. And I understand their point intellectually and I have had experiences that revolved around gender differences and the dominance of men in authority positions. But I can't really identify with that sort of discussion because my father was such an influential force in my life. Any self-doubt I had in life was mitigated by my father's belief that I could do anything in the world I wanted to. To this day, that belief gives me an overwhelming sense of comfort and strength. My hope is that I can provide that same support to my own daughter as she grows and matures."

BIBLIOGRAPHICAL NOTE

Sarita Brown's story derives from multiple sources. Included in the list are interview transcripts, her curriculum vitae, the *Excelencia* in Education's website at http://www.edexcelencia.org, and various *Excelencia* research reports and policy briefs.

three

LIFE'S CHALLENGES AND THE MEANING OF SUCCESS

Tina Cordova

IN 1990 WITH $5,000 IN SAVINGS, thirty-one-year-old Tina Cordova started a roofing company with her partner, Russ Steward. Queston Construction is a family-run operation. Her father, son, brothers, nephew, and cousins have all worked for the company at one time or another. It was converted from a general partnership between Cordova and Steward to a corporation in 1999, with Tina as president and CEO. The focus of the firm is commercial and residential construction and all types of roofing. The Albuquerque enterprise has grown from a two-person (Cordova and Steward) firm to one with thirty year-round full-time employees and a multimillion-dollar revenue stream. Today it is one of New Mexico's largest and most successful roofing companies—so successful, in fact, that Tina received the 1998 Entrepreneur of the Year award from New Mexico's Small Business Administration and the 2000 U.S. Small Business Administration's Small Business Person of the Year award for New Mexico.

"Family is central to my success. My only son, David, is grown now, has finished college, and is working for the company. It can be difficult supervising him," she laughs, "but I have been supervising him his whole life! The great thing about working with David is that he is extremely bright. Whenever I need an objective opinion, he is the one I go to. He has been that way for me most of my life. Once he got to a certain age I could discuss issues and concerns with him. We work well together. I hope that he will eventually replace me as president of the company. I am grooming him for that job.

"It's never easy having family work for you, but it does give you the opportunity to help family when they need it. And, they give back to us; they pitch in and work hard. We have a relationship that works. I never expect any of them to work here forever. I always think of it as a stepping-stone for them into something else. For example, one of my younger brothers lost his job. He worked for us for a couple of years and then found a job in his own line of work. And, I laugh a lot about the time my dad worked here. I always teased him about coming and going as he pleased and doing what he wanted. I did it in jest because he worked very hard for us right up to the time he retired. If you think it's hard supervising your son, try your father!

"I grew up in Tularosa, New Mexico, in a strong Catholic family. Most of my ancestors were born in New Mexico when it was still part of Mexico. You know the history. Most of what is now New Mexico, Texas, Arizona, and California was once part of Mexico. I tell people that it's not that my family *came* here. They *were* here. It's just that the border moved. New Mexico is very unique that way. Many of us here can trace our ancestry back several hundred years.

"My parents graduated from high school but never attended college. My mother worked at home until we were all in school and then developed a career as a property appraiser. My father managed a grocery store. There were less than five thousand people in the town where I grew up. Everybody knew everybody. I was particularly close to my grandparents. We all lived together, including my aunts and uncles. I never considered myself poor because nobody else was rich. We had what we needed. We didn't want for much.

"When I was growing up we ate dinner together every night. We never missed. My parents made sure that we had time to discuss our activities in school and how we were doing. They were very involved; they monitored us closely and supported our efforts to excel. We were raised to believe that we could do whatever we set our minds to but that we should do so with regard and respect for those around us. There were no boundaries placed on me. I grew up hearing that I could succeed if I really wanted to.

"In fact, my parents were adamant about all four of us (I am the oldest) getting a good education and going to college. We all went to college or trade school. My younger brother and I have master's degrees. Both of my degrees are from New Mexico Highlands University.

"My family, the family that raised me, is a significant part of who I am. I am proud of my Hispanic heritage. My first language is English and I am fairly fluent in Spanish, and being bilingual is a real benefit in the business world. My father's early education suffered because of his lack of English-language skills. His extended family spoke Spanish, and my parents' generation was disciplined at school for speaking Spanish.

"In those days there was such a push to speak only English, and a great deal of racism existed in our little town. The village was settled entirely by Hispanics. As Anglos moved in, they took over. They gained wealth very quickly and they ran everything. My dad tells a story about his grandfather who worked as a ranch hand for a businessman in town. He worked for him for forty years and the day he passed away they didn't even acknowledge that he'd died. Those experiences had a huge impact on my father. He decided that we all had to be proficient in English. We spoke only English at home. Our parents insisted on it. My father always said: 'You have to learn English first and if you learn Spanish later, that's fine.'

"My mother spoke nothing but English until she married my father. Then she learned Spanish. I learned it in school and later through my work, not at home. What I find so interesting now is that most schoolchildren—like my grandson Demetrius—spend half the school day speaking Spanish and the other half, English. He is incredibly proficient in both; and I am proud of the fact that we are recovering our language. It is part of our culture.

"As individuals, we take our culture with us, and cultural differences can be significant. For instance, I employ several Mexican immigrants. U.S.-born Mexican and Mexican-born individuals have cultural differences. These differences guide how I interact with them. I need to understand what is significant to each one of them. Each of us has qualities that are useful. We need to identify those values and strengths and weaknesses. I delegate tasks based on what I think a person can bring to a situation. I once owned a restaurant that employed a male dishwasher who liked working with customers. I said to him, 'I want you to get drink orders and serve chips and salsa during the busy time.' He was great with the customers. As a result, he gained self-confidence, and customers came back to the restaurant.

"One of the most important differences between Mexican and U.S.-born Mexicans is education. U.S.-born Mexicans are educated in the U.S.; they are proficient with the English language, know where to go to get the information needed, and how to mobilize resources. I am a fifth- or sixth-generation Hispanic born in this country. I have had the advantage of education. I understand very well. I know how to acquire the information and knowledge that I need and what to do with it once I have it. I have a certain level of confidence because I don't face those barriers that can result from a lack of these skills. I didn't have to focus my attention on getting, doing, and keeping a job; I could have a career. When people immigrate here they are not part of that learning process. They might be very proficient in their country and their language, but here it is a whole different story. It's one of the things that sets us apart.

"In a male-dominated field like construction, gender also sets us apart. But, my extensive knowledge of roofing and the construction industry generally causes others to respect my opinion. I have had some challenges. One time I went to speak with a university maintenance person. I explained how a particular roof would be best for the school; it would save money and last longer. He was set in his ways and said, 'Lady, I wouldn't buy that roof from you if you danced in a bathing suit on top of that desk.' I replied, 'You know what, I've never done that before and I don't ever plan to. If you were smart you'd listen to what I'm telling you and you'd save your university a whole lot of money.' Then I picked up my stuff and left. I never did work there.

"It boils down to competency. Women, especially, must possess the intelligence and mental capacity to fully understand the business they are in and be able to work under pressure to get the job done right. A woman who wants to be successful must be incredibly competent at what she does, see the big picture but stay focused on getting from point A to point B, and be strong-willed enough to get it done. Particularly, if she's in a field that is dominated by men. You simply *have* to know what you're doing.

"I have a master's in biology and was in medical school. I became a single mom after a divorce and had to leave school. I immediately found a job in the restaurant business and worked my way up into management. I left that job to start Queston.

When I began soliciting business, I continually had to demon-strate my competence. But being competent worked. It gave me credibility. Today, I tell my assistant that if she gets a call about a roofing system or the specifics of a job, to refer it to me. I know my business and I've made absolutely certain I know my busi-ness better than anyone else. Often men tell me: 'I've talked to all sorts of people, almost all of them men, and no one knows as much as you do about construction and roofing.' I've learned to become very good at what I do so that people don't ever treat me with disrespect.

"I am resilient and have the physical stamina to press forward. I know that I must look for ways to communicate what it is that I believe our customer needs and what it is we can deliver. I rarely take 'no' for an answer. When someone says 'no' to me I think, 'Okay, they're just not seeing it the way I see it.' When one person doesn't view a situation the way I do, I go to others so I know that I'm getting my point across and am being treated fairly. One time I had a contract with the state of New Mexico. The architect supervisor of the contract was unreasonable about the work we had completed. Finally I said, 'That is it.' I went to the lieutenant governor's office to find out who supervised him. The state sent a third party to investigate the situation and I was paid the final payment.

"It's also about perseverance. I've received many contracts be-cause I was able to stay in the game, fight, and win! I truly believe that if you spend enough hours at something, you'll succeed. I started this construction company even though I didn't know much about roofing. I did know that if I failed, I'd have to go to work for someone else. I worked hard, I learned, I persevered, and I succeeded.

"For me, success means that I have the freedom to make choices about what I spend my time doing. If I get a call from my brother and he says he needs me to pick up his girls, I can say, 'No problem, I'll take care of it.' I don't have to ask anybody for permission. I have the financial freedom to be able to call all sorts of shots. If I want to take off tomorrow, I can do it. If I find a compelling cause and I decide to send a check to some foundation because they need help, well, I just do it.

"A decade or more ago, my view of success was not the same as it is today. Back then, I was very focused on becoming "successful" and that meant, for the most part, financial independence. But in 1998, I was diagnosed with thyroid cancer and my entire worldview changed.

"Having cancer refocused in a significant way how I look at life. Now I really do understand what's important and what's not. It was a blessing in some ways. I feel comfortable in who I am and how life has evolved for me. When you're young and naïve, you think that life should be a certain way and that success is defined as having 'x.' It is not reality. It's just not. With cancer I came to understand life differently and I'm so grateful for having had that experience. Today, I consider every morning I wake up a direct gift from God. Simply put, I am a faith-filled woman who is very dedicated to her family and to her work.

"I also like to work in the community. For instance, I helped form a group that focuses on getting Latinas more politically active in their communities. I take pride in analyzing situations and helping others solve problems. I have been asked by chairmen of boards and company presidents for advice. People know I am reflective. In a group when presented with a task, I immediately ask myself, 'How would I approach this issue?'

"I advocate for Hispanic workers and businesses. I keep active. I am a Type-A personality and have been that way since I was a child. I get up at 6:30 a.m., spend half an hour in my garden, and then get ready for work. Because I love to cook, I do some of the preparation for dinner before leaving for the office. I am at work by nine and work straight through until five or six in the evening. Once home, I fix dinner, walk the dog, make telephone calls, write a few e-mails, and read the newspaper. I rarely turn on the television except to watch the late-night news and am in bed by eleven.

"I live with my significant other and business partner, which is actually much more challenging than working with the rest of my family. It's very difficult to separate our business from our personal lives. When we do have a chance to go out for dinner or to a movie, I have to say: 'Okay, we're *not* going to talk about business tonight!' We have to make these kinds of deals together or else we'd talk about business 100 percent of the time.

"When I can get away, I go fishing. People probably think that's crazy. But it's so good for me because it forces me to slow down and be patient. I love the outdoors and the water. I like being in the sun. If I catch a fish, well, great." She laughs. "I'd much rather be at the lake fishing and camping than at the mall shopping.

"I don't take many days off, no vacation. People call me a workaholic. I am very passionate about my business. It becomes personal when your company is small and consumes all of your time. People depend on me to feed their families. One year I gave a company Christmas party for employees and their families to which 160 people came. I was able to see the company all together. I saw the children's faces. It was overwhelming, knowing they all count on me. I take it very, very seriously. I constantly look for opportunities and bring my 'just do it' spirit to the table, but I don't ask anyone to do anything I won't do myself.

"I recently began developing a succession plan for the business. I thought I'd worked out a good plan that involved the closest members of my family. Then, in 2008 my nephew passed away. He was twenty-three years old. I helped raise him; he was my godson. It was devastating for me. In fact, the year following his death was the hardest year of my life. It was very hard to continue doing what I did each day because he was such a big part of my daily work life. Probably 90 percent of the time, his was the first call I got every morning. We organized the day together. He and I worked closely in managing the residential side of our business. It's been a tremendous struggle for me. His loss created such a great void.

"I work in a tough environment and had always prided myself on not crying at work. I never shed a tear. But during that year there were many times I had to close my door because I just broke down. In general, I had a very difficult time motivating myself. But somehow I managed to and have come to realize that life goes on. I am still here, we are all still here, and we have to continue. This was the turning point for me. I had faced challenges before—being a teenage mother, a divorcee, a single mother, a cancer survivor, having to change my career plans—but I had never faced a challenge like this one. I will forever measure time against his death. We haven't been able to imagine replacing him. We simply absorbed the work that he had done.

"I am very strong in my Catholic faith. That faith brings with it a kind of peace, reconciliation, and optimism. I have come to understand that the sun will rise tomorrow, no matter what, and that things work out in the end. I try not to fret for very long when plans go awry and I try to learn from my mistakes. The challenges we face only make us wiser and stronger in the long run. Family and faith have taught me that."

BIBLIOGRAPHICAL NOTE

Tina Cordova's story is taken from many readings of formal interview transcripts intertwined with materials from informal conversations, e-mail exchanges, her résumé, and her website, http://www.queston.net.

four

SUCCESS, THE NAME OF THE QUEST

Sally Garza Fernandez

S ALLY GARZA FERNANDEZ is the president of The Fernandez Group; chief executive officer of Fernandez Enterprises; president of Safety Dynamics, Inc.; founder of the Technology Development and Research Institute; and a partner of Unmanned Vehicle Technologies. It all started in 1996. Sally was thirty-eight and her daughter, Marti, was thirteen when she left the corporate world to start her own consulting business in Tucson, Arizona.

"I went into business for myself primarily because I wanted to have more time with my daughter. I was so busy with my career I felt I hardly knew her. The question for me was, 'What am I doing with my life?' I felt there simply had to be a better way, so I started The Fernandez Group, which today includes manufacturing and distribution companies as well as the original consulting business."

Fernandez Enterprises distributes maintenance equipment for aircraft, ground vehicles, and watercraft in military, homeland security, and commercial markets. Safety Dynamics, Inc., develops, designs, and markets temporal pattern recognition products to federal government agencies, law enforcement, and municipalities. Safety Dynamics' products lead the industry as the fastest, most accurate portable smart sensor systems for use in the world of security.

Small economical, portable, lightweight, unmanned air vehicles that can support a wide variety of operations, such as surveillance, tracking of targets, and reconnaissance, are designed and marketed by Unmanned Vehicle Technologies, LLC. Technology Development and Research Institute (TDRI) offers shared resources to technology-based companies to facilitate the development of new technologies/products that support commercial, defense, and homeland and border security needs. Its secondary mission is to provide an industry-designed, practical application learning environment for underrepresented minority youth, particularly Native American and Hispanic. Its purpose is to pique their interest in science, math, and engineering.

The consulting arm of The Fernandez Group advises companies in Mexico, the United States, and Canada in the areas of organizational development, crisis management, marketing and advertising, and transition planning. In total, Sally oversees an enterprise that employs over fifty professionals (many of them researchers) at any given time. Experts suggest that the total worth of all of Fernandez's interests will top typical small-business growth rates over the next several years.[1]

Sally has been married since 1996 to attorney Douglas Zirkle, who serves as the Fernandez Group's general counsel. Her

---

1. In 2007 and 2008 Fernandez was recognized by the Tucson Metropolitan Chamber of Commerce as the Small Business Leader of the Year. In 2007 she was named Manufacturer of the Year by the Microbusiness Advancement Center and Small Business Alliance of Southern Arizona. The previous year the Tucson Hispanic Chamber of Commerce honored her as the Hispanic Business Woman of the Year.

daughter also works with her. Her two older sons had embarked on their career paths prior to the inception of Fernandez's endeavors.

"I was raised in Port Huron, Michigan, a typical, all-American, predominantly Anglo community. My grandfather came to the U.S. in the 1920s. He was a lawyer who upon arrival in the U.S. founded the Mexican Credit Union. My father was a skilled tradesman with journeymen's status as a machinist and welder. My mother was a bank manager.

"My parents were very proficient in Spanish and English. When my sister, who is eight years older than I am, was little my parents spoke both Spanish and English at home. After I was born, they spoke only English. My grandfather felt strongly that we needed to understand and speak English fluently. He believed that it would make us successful. I took Spanish in high school but also picked up an understanding of the language at home because my grandmother lived with us for some time and she only spoke Spanish.

"Growing up, I was one of those kids who was always involved, five years old and staying after school to help the teacher. The signs were there very early on. I was kind of 'out there.' I was pretty self-reliant. My daughter, Marti, behaves exactly the same way. I don't know if it is a learned behavior or an inherited one. I used to tell people when she was young that all I had to do was give her a lunch box and the key to the house and she was good to go. She's still a lot like me.

"I'm not overly outgoing, but as a youngster I was not shy when I was around adults or classmates. In high school I was active in student government and cheerleading. I was on the debate team and student council. I was very involved. I felt I had to be, that I was preparing myself to succeed in the future. This is important for young people to understand because involvement can be a key to success. Being involved opens options—points to possibilities. For example, I participated in the Explorers program in Junior Achievement. It introduced me to law as a profession and sparked an interest in me. Other high school activities afforded me the opportunity to observe different leadership and speaking styles. If I had not had these experiences, I would only know what my family could show and tell me. I broadened my horizons and extended my baseline of knowledge through my high school activities. They definitely helped shape who I am today. Over the years, I encouraged my daughter to do the same.

"When I was in high school I decided I wanted to study political science and maybe go on to law school. I wanted to go to a good college. One of the school counselors told me, 'You'll never be accepted to the kind of university you want to attend,' even though I was in the Honor Society and had good grades. Apparently he didn't think they were good enough. I thought he was wrong, and his attitude only made me more determined to succeed. I went to the assistant principal and asked him to write a letter of support for me. He was very helpful. I was accepted at all the places I applied.

"I attended Michigan State University and earned my political science and pre-law degree in 1980 and then participated in postgraduate studies in public administration at the University of Michigan and in law at the Detroit College of Law until a career change sent me to St. Louis, Missouri. As bright as my parents were, they had not attended college so they couldn't help me. I learned how to be successful at college on my own. I have had to figure out life by myself.

"I've worked for General Motors, Anheuser-Busch, and Hughes Missile System. Each move proved to be a turning point in my career. In 1982, when I was twenty-four, I was hired by the General Motors Corporation in Detroit to help them figure out

how to survive a boycott by the Hispanic community. I re-
searched the issues and developed a road map for how to reposi-
tion the company in the Hispanic market. It was a big job.
Eventually, I moved into the executive development program and
then on to the advanced engineering staff. When I was twenty-
nine, I left Detroit and went to work for Anheuser-Busch in St.
Louis, Missouri, where I was the director of corporate relations
and responsible for the worldwide Hispanic, Asian, and American Indian markets. I was one of twenty women among two hundred Anheuser-Busch executives.

"At thirty-four, I left Anheuser-Busch and became part of the
executive team for the Weapons Systems Segment Group at
Hughes Missile Systems in Tucson. The company had become
the target of a negative campaign about contaminating ground-
water. I was hired to deal with the situation. It seems like I was
always hired to go in and solve one problem or another. My jobs
have always demanded that I be highly visible.

"There have been times when I've accomplished something
that I didn't think I was capable of doing. I never thought I could
do the job at General Motors, but I did. Getting the position at
Anheuser-Busch was a big deal because I was the youngest Hispanic female executive in the company's history. I was suddenly
eligible for stock options and bonuses and all kinds of things that
I thought only men got.

"Now I own five successful companies [The Fernandez
Group]. Getting my first company up and running was probably
the biggest step forward. When I decided to go out on my own, I
began by cleaning out my old corporate files that I'd stored in the
garage. I saw my true passion there in all of them—the drive to
solve problems, to build, to succeed. That discovery started my
entrepreneurial career.

"I've worked very hard at it. I've put a great deal of sweat and tears into each and every business. The Fernandez Group is a limited liability company. I am the only member. Some of the individual companies do have shareholders who should fare very well if they ever choose to sell their holdings because I continually reinvest in them.

"I don't ask my staff to do anything I wouldn't do. I might be at home in Tucson, get up and be in Washington by seven, then travel that same afternoon to Chicago and on to Tulsa or Baltimore in the evening. I put my heart into whatever I do. I commit my time and energy, and I push ahead. I ask, 'Where is the organization going? How do we get where we need to be?' And I reflect on the answers to those questions every day. I make a list of the things I want to accomplish. Is there a book I want to read? A proposal I want to write? I document everything. I hold myself accountable.

"Certain principles guide me in my work world. These principles revolve around credibility, competence, discipline and focus, passion, confidence, communication, culture, humility and balance in life, and self-improvement.

"Credibility is crucial. You must live up to your word. Competence is a mainstay of credibility. Although I am a talented businessperson, I have no technical credentials. Yet I deal with individuals with technical doctoral degrees and I am able to command credibility. How do I do that? I read books and periodicals. I frequently scan the environment and think about how a particular circumstance impacts my company. For example, I might have decided that our product is X, but at the same time I seek out other opportunities. You must think strategically and clearly present your assessment of various situations. Possibilities can be esoteric and you might not readily see them. You must continually reflect on what you are doing and what is going on around you so that you can move your vision beyond what it is today, even if at the time it is not possible to totally understand it.

"One of the most important building blocks for a successful business career is discipline and focus. In my experience, successful businesses set goals that are focused and establish metrics to measure their performance. Because our environment evolves continually this process is repeated over and over again.

"To be successful, leaders need to both engage and enable people around them. People get excited because of the passion effective leaders demonstrate. Leaders who have a 'roll up your sleeves' kind of attitude typically don't fail because those around them know that they are willing to dive in at every level and do what they require of their peers. This approach is engaging, and it demonstrates humility and respect for others.

"I am confident. From a very young age, I've known that when I walk in to do a job I have to look in charge. I present myself in a strong way, but not so strong that I intimidate people. I have to believe in whatever I'm doing. I often advise other companies on how to deal with environmental issues. I've told leaders of these companies: 'If you're not sincere about truly changing your business practices, then there's no reason for me to be here.'

"It's also essential that you be a great communicator, a task that has become increasingly complex with the advent of technology. Personally, I like the old-fashioned way. I simply pick up the telephone and begin a dialogue. It's critical for me to engage with people and make absolutely certain I understand them and they understand me.

"Whether or not you learn and understand the intricacies of an organization's culture can determine whether or not you succeed or fail. Culture is something that needs to be read day to day. Personal perception plays an intimate role. I'm the kind of person who tends to see the glass half full; others see it half empty. It makes a difference. For example, at Safety Dynamics the ideas seemed disconnected when I first came on the scene. So, I had to understand the environment based on my own experience and my own learning from people I admire, such as [author/consultant] Jim Collins. When I am in these types of situations, I become a sponge and I absorb everything. I try to focus on perceptions and subtleties. I learned from a CEO at General Motors what *not* to do. He lacked focus and was a poor communicator. As a result, people who worked under him were not as engaged as they should have been. In contrast, August Busch III created a very special culture at Anheuser-Busch. He engrained in the organization several values: cleanliness, pride, and quality. I remember my first job interview. The sidewalks were clean and shiny. You could eat off of them. That was a unique culture.

"It is important to not take yourself too seriously, to have balance in your life. The world is not all about you. You need to look around and ask yourself: What have I done today for others that is good? My family has always given back to our community by helping those in need. I have witnessed my family doing some type of charity work my entire life. We must determine what is valuable in life, what is truly important.

"I learn something new every day. It's like being in a constant mode of continuing education—some self-taught, some with the aid of others. I think there is room for women in the technology arena, but we all (men and women alike) need guidance and coaching on how to be truly successful. I had a great mentor [in] Stan Abrams. He joined me in my first consulting contract. He taught me to have courage and helped me during the first five years of being in private business. It was all about me and what I could do to inspire trust in people. Today, people trust me; they trust what I say.

"Events in my personal life have greatly impacted my professional one. Perhaps the biggest event of them all was being pregnant and having my daughter, Marti. Although Marti was born in 1983, it wasn't until I started my own company in 1996 that I really felt like I was a mom. Prior to that time, I was too busy working. That's why I decided on such a huge career change, to be able to spend more time with her. In addition, the internal competitiveness was getting old. I had faced discrimination issues because I am Hispanic. I dealt with sexual harassment, backstabbing, and the politicking that happens between peers. Going into business on my own worked out very well for me.

"My second marriage was also a very big turning point in my life. My children are grown and, quite frankly, my two grandchildren have added a wonderful dynamic to our lives. I love my grandchildren. I recently spent time with them, and it reminded me of just how much I value them. I want to have more time with them. Watching my daughter, Marti, evolve in the business world has also been important. It has been a challenge for me to learn how exactly to coach and mentor her. Mentoring your own child is a lot harder than mentoring somebody else. She's a business partner of mine in two of our family-owned businesses. One, Aniko Salon and Spa in Chicago, is particularly exciting because it took me out of my comfort zone. In 2007, the business we purchased had three part-time employees serving about 330 customers a month. Today we have thirty employees and nearly 1,000 regular customers. Marti runs the day-to-day operations. We talk on the phone nearly every day and, for the most part, half of the conversation is about business and the other half is personal. Once a month I travel to Chicago for staff meetings. It can be interesting to work with family in a business because you have to find a balance.

"Watching my parents grow old has been a difficult time for me. With children you know they're going to grow up and all those goofy things they're doing are going to stop. With parents—particularly those with dementia—it's just the opposite. It doesn't get better, only worse. My parents needed so much care that I knew I needed help. Just that realization was hard for me. I looked for months for the right place to put them but wasn't happy with any of the facilities I saw. Of course, that was because I am their daughter and nothing was going to be good enough for my parents. I finally found the perfect spot. Many of the staff members are Hispanic and the entire facility is run with a sense of warmth, grace, dignity, and charm. I am happy with our choice.

"I think I must be at a weird point in my life where everything begins to happen all at once. My husband was recently diagnosed with prostate cancer. My daughter just got married. It took me a long time to accept that now she's not only my daughter but also someone else's wife.

"Maybe I worry too much. I've always been an achiever. I've always been very entrepreneurial, like my father and grandfather before me. Even though my four siblings work hard and some own businesses, I am the extreme overachiever. More determined, more focused, more disciplined. I have made sacrifices, but I have also gained great rewards.

"I work very hard to ensure my success. I'm usually up between six and seven in the morning and at the office shortly after that. I tend to go right to my computer to see what happened the day before and then begin to work instantly on all the stuff I need to do. Sometime in the course of the morning I get a cup of tea and take my vitamins; I work nonstop for three hours and then I try to work out. I'm gone for about two hours, exercising for one hour and relaxing in the Jacuzzi and stretching for the other hour. Then it's back to the office, more work, lunch, and work until about 3 or 3:30 in the afternoon, when I visit my parents for about an hour. Back to the office for another couple of hours, and finally home for dinner. I'm in bed by nine. My weekends sound much the same. I end up doing errands and cleaning around the house and I work out and I see my parents. I work two to four hours on company business each day on the weekend. So, I generally work seven days a week.

"Even if I'd like more time to myself, I'm not thinking of retiring any time soon. In fact, I don't ever see myself retiring. I will probably always have a little bit of work at the companies I have an interest in and perhaps do more volunteer work as time passes. I want to write a book about all my varied business experiences. And my daughter and I are working on an outline for a reality TV show designed to help mothers and daughters in family businesses learn from our experiences. Such dreams! I will always be learning. I might take classes or learn another language. I'll play with my grandchildren. I won't ever just become stagnant. Even now, I have hobbies. I like to golf." Laughingly, she says, "You know, now that I think about it, I haven't been golfing in ten years! And I live on the golf course. In fact, we've lived on three different golf courses.

"In the end, it's all about being and staying successful. And what *is* success? Simply put, happiness. Happiness is balance in my life, having sufficient time for my family, sufficient time for myself, sufficient time for my businesses. It comes down to having enough time to do all the things that are important to me. For me, happiness, success, and balance have become intricately intertwined."

BIBLIOGRAPHICAL NOTE

The story of Sally Garza Fernandez evolved from a series of interviews, e-mail exchanges, and her résumé. The following websites were also examined: Paragon Space Development at www.para gonsdc.com, Hispanic Enterprise at www.hispaniconline.com/ HE/2008.01/Feature-S&M.html, Sally Fernandez Garza at www .tucsoncitizen.com, and Aniko Salon and Spa at www.aniko salonspa.com. One additional company in The Fernandez Group, Safety Dynamics, has an official website, but The Fernandez Group itself does not have one.

five

FIGHTING THE GOOD
FIGHT AND WINNING

Carmella Franco

"Dr. Darline Robles, my dear colleague, and I are about the same age (I'm fifty-nine; she's a year older) and have similar backgrounds.[1] We both grew up in east Los Angeles. And, we both like boxing. She had well-known boxer Oscar de la Hoya in her neighborhood; I had Armando Muníz in mine. My great-uncle had a boxing ring for the youth in the community. He also was an accomplished pianist. I used to go down to the ring and watch them spar and read the boxing magazines. Every Saturday my father took me to my piano lessons. We'd drive to the music school, and then on the way home we'd stop at the Olympic Auditorium, where some well-known boxers used to spar, including Art Aragon, the Golden Boy (he was a Golden Gloves champion, hence the nickname). It's interesting that one great-uncle had such a dramatic dual influence, music and boxing, on me as he did.

[1] Darline Robles's story is featured in chapter 8.

"Darline and I also share similar career paths—teacher, principal, personnel, and superintendent. As we progressed through our careers, we both developed the skills and strategies needed to work with oppositional forces, especially those with a political edge. I learned many lessons from boxing—carefully study the opposition, obtain the necessary training (education and degrees), strategize and focus on successful techniques, watch for surprise moves, know when to be on the offense and when to be on the defense, rebound from any knockouts, pick your battles selectively, and don't be afraid to fight for what you believe in. Bob and weave. Bob and weave. Those lessons colored my dissertation topic—nontraditional negotiation methods—and to this day, my approach to leadership. One of my board members once got really upset about what he called 'the blood and gore,' referring to what went on in meetings. I said, 'It's not gore. It's the strategy,' meaning being tough.

"I was born in Colorado but the family relocated in southern California early on. As a child, I was in a school that was 99 percent Hispanic. My father was an automobile mechanic with the police department, and my mother went to college and became an RN in her early forties. I was the eldest of six children, three boys and three girls. All of us went to college, and two of us obtained advanced degrees. Until I was five, we lived in the same house with my maternal grandparents in Colorado. After moving to Los Angeles, we bought three houses on a lot from my paternal grandparents. Although we no longer had extended family living with us, all of our social time was spent with family. I had twenty-one first cousins, and several were not only family, but dear friends. My paternal grandmother was a tremendous influence in my life. She had faced hard times and adversity and was as strong as steel, yet she was a loving and kind soul. In seventh grade we moved to a nicer area, in the suburbs, where half the class was Anglo. The only commonality I had with the other students was that we were all strong academically. We were high achievers. Even then, all of us had ambitions to do well in high school and to go on to college.

"In school, my Latina identity was not the thing that stood out. However, as I moved on in my career, having learned my ethnic language, Spanish, opened many doors. I became involved with CABE, the California Association of Bilingual Education. As time went on, because I was a bilingual teacher, I became a principal who was also bilingual and then a director in a school district that had a sizeable Cuban population. I'm not Cuban, but I was able to communicate well with that community. When I was named superintendent in Whittier City, the board said that I met all the criteria, but the icing on the cake was that I could speak Spanish and connect with the community. Those experiences really put it in perspective for me, that my being Latina and my ability to speak my family language had been assets throughout my life.

"I served as superintendent in Whittier City School District [California] for twelve years, culminating over thirty-six years of educational service to children, and then began immediately as interim superintendent for Woodland Joint Unified School District in the summer of 2008. Woodland Unified serves almost eleven thousand students in seventeen schools and has an operating budget of just under $100 million. I went from a day of retiring on July 31 to starting officially in this interim position on August 1.

"My passion for the superintendency has grown over time. I could not be doing what I'm doing right now without absolutely loving what I do and knowing that what I do is making a difference. I'm facilitating the improvement of education and learning for our students. I have felt that way about every single position that I have held. As I moved through the positions, I had that absolute love for what I was doing. I gave my all, gave 150 percent. I hated to leave each position because each was so exciting to me."

Carmella Franco earned her bachelor of arts degree in music and her master of arts in elementary education from California State University, Los Angeles. Her doctorate in educational management was from the University of La Verne. She spent the first five years of her educational career teaching elementary school and then moved to the central office, where she became a bilingual specialist. Elementary and middle school principalships followed, with a central office position as director of certificated and classified personnel serving as her step to the superintendent's office. She has also served on the boards of numerous professional organizations—Association of Latino Administrators and Superintendents, Association of California School Administrators Regions (ACSA) 14 and 15, California Latino Superintendents Association, and Southern Counties Women in Educational Management, to name a few. A true educator at heart, Franco has taught educational management courses at California State University, Los Angeles and presented workshops inside and outside education. Numerous awards cover her walls including the Hispanic Outreach Taskforce's Positive Image Award in Education and California Congresswoman Grace Napolitano's Woman of the Year Award.

"I'm a demanding leader. I want the best for the students. So, from every department I expect the best, and I'm not very tolerant of that not occurring. I have strong beliefs about what I want to see in my district, but there needs to be a collective vision and a collective collaboration in carrying out that vision. Everyone must want to do his or her best.

"One of the most important strategies for establishing a collective vision is adequate professional preparation. I always made sure that I was fully prepared, or as prepared as I could be, not knowing the exact details of the position. I went about it very methodically just like a boxer does—always in training. I learned that if you lack experience in a specific area, you need to develop a good hold of it some other way. There were two programs that helped me most. One was my doctoral program. We were put through scenario after scenario designed to expose us to the complexities of being a school superintendent. I applied everything that I learned in that program and nothing was a surprise.

"The second program was the ACSA Superintendent's Academy for aspiring superintendents, which I now direct. That program covers the politics of the role using real-life stories and demonstrations to lay it all out so that those who really have the superintendency as a goal are ready for it. It includes the whole realm of dealing with the board, staff, parents, and the community at large, including businesses and people who do not have school-age children. Even so, nothing really prepares you for the politics that can develop once you are a superintendent. During my thirty-one years as an administrator, I attended board meetings up to three times a month. But, not until I was sitting in the superintendent's seat did I truly realize what the politics entail. You have to think about every angle of any decision because it has the potential to stir up trouble. I always liked politics and I think it has been positive for me."

At the time Franco was superintendent, Whittier City School District served seven thousand students in thirteen schools with over eight hundred employees. As she aptly put it, "I confidently stepped into that ring in 1996, looking for a win. Oh, that was a great time! I walked into a meeting where the board approved a bond. We were going to be the first district in the area to go after about $9 million. We had three major projects—class-size reduction, outside building maintenance, and technology infrastructure. I knew nothing about going after a bond, but I learned. I was out in the community forty-three of forty-six nights straight, between when I started August 1 and the bond election in November of that year. I met everyone, and while it was a whirlwind way to do it, it was invaluable. It gave me a jump on the game. I had a number of key people from town take me around to meet everyone. I spoke at all the service clubs, and the following year I was asked to be on a number of boards in town. Those kinds of connections with the business community were good for me and for the district. The bond barely passed, but we did pass it. You need to start with a win. If that bond had failed, I would have started off with a losing legacy. It would have colored everything. To this day I cringe at the thought of such a loss.

"We needed to build seven multipurpose rooms, redo all underground utilities at a major cost, and paint every building. That was one of the best things we did. I've always said, as much as the classroom is the center of the universe, people don't drive by the classroom, they drive by the outside of a school and they see whether it's maintained and what's fairly newly painted and looks good. We bought beautiful playground equipment for every elementary school, and we made sure it went in first, so something was visible to each school community. Then we started the building of the multipurpose rooms, and we did a lot of infrastructure work with technology. I had a good opening to my first months in Whittier City. When we started, we promised the community that if we finished the three projects, and they liked all three of them, that we'd come back for a larger bond because we had other things to do. Two and a half years later, we passed another bond.

"You also have to know how to shape your battles. At Woodland Joint Unified School District, I walked into a situation where there was a major brouhaha going on over the district music program. I spent a couple of weeks assessing the situation. I looked at the master schedule, comparing class offerings at the different secondary schools, middle school to middle school, high school to high school, so that I could see what was happening. It turned out that there indeed was an inequity in one of the strands while all other schools were doing fine. It was the only weakness in the program. I took a proposal to my very first board meeting but didn't ask them to act on it. Instead I told them I was going to present it, and if they had no objections, I was going to implement it. Basically I turned the table around. If the board had acted on it, they would be admitting that they were not properly supporting our district music program. What I did was identify some glitches in the program and tell them how we were going to correct them. There were over two hundred people in the audience and everyone expected it to be delayed and postponed, but I took care of it right there, with five recommendations. Because music was a major interest for everyone in town, the stage was set for me to come in on a win. With my music background it was just perfect.

"At Woodland, I came in running just as hard as I had at Whittier. I was out speaking to groups right off and attending as many programs out in the schools as I could. I went to nearly every back-to-school night at the seventeen schools in August and September. Some were on the same nights. I ran from one to the other. I attended music programs with large audiences. I worked closely with the board.

"I was on the offense, but leaders also need to know when to be on the defense. You have to be able to roll with the punches and hope they don't result in knockouts. In my first three to four weeks at Woodland, we had three key people leave—the director of pupil services; the associate superintendent of educational services; and my assistant, who was promoted to a classified management position at a good-sized salary increase. They followed the prior superintendent to her new district. While most would have found the situation daunting, I looked for the silver lining. I found that new opportunities and new doors opened for the district.

"Whittier had different issues. A major challenge there was declining enrollment, in fact six years of decline accompanied by annual budget reductions and cuts, which were very debilitating and demoralizing. We just did not have money. I worked like crazy with staff to bring in over $12 million in grants during that time. If we had not had those grants, we would have had a shell of a school system. We had music grants, art grants, technology grants, writing grants, and a huge Twenty-First Century after-school grant. Our kids had wonderful programs and experiences as a result. To the end of my superintendency, money was a formidable obstacle, but we dealt with it.

"Another obstacle at Whittier had to do with the low expectations that some teachers held regarding what students could achieve. In one school where even though all of its teachers were fully qualified per both No Child Left Behind and the California guidelines for credentialing, they didn't push their students to perform academically. That one school stood out like a sore thumb.

"We wanted to close the achievement gap between this school and the others in the district. We paired all schools to look at student work and student writing. We matched the subpar school up with the highest-achieving school. They didn't realize what we were doing. We knew the issue was easy grading. Teachers from both schools in each pair of schools graded student work in both schools. They used a six-point rubric for writing and the same student writing samples. The exercise highlighted the problem. If the high-achieving schoolteachers gave a piece of work a score of three, the low-achieving schoolteachers were likely to award the same paper a score of five or six.

"A culture that promoted accepting the way things were had set in at the low-achieving school. I went through those classrooms, and I was appalled at what I saw. I set a Saturday and met the principal, the assistant superintendent of business, and maintenance personnel at the school with big trash bins. We went room to room and I said, 'Throw this out, throw that out.' The kindergarten room had painting easels with broken legs that were just propped against the wall. We cleared those rooms of junk and trash. Monday morning I immediately got a call from the teachers' union: 'Was it true I had gone through their classrooms?' The word spread like wildfire. I said, 'Yes,' and I promised to replace the broken-down items that were thrown out from my own office budget.

"Then I met with the staff. I approached them with an offer of help. I asked, 'What isn't working at the school? What do you need? What's holding us back?' Twenty-six things went up on the flip charts—all having to do with facilities. The fronts of the rooms were painted brown. 'Too dark,' they said. So we painted them a creamy white. There was an overhang outside the whole front of the school that darkened the rooms. I had it torn off, and the stucco mended. We took care of all twenty-six concerns.

"A couple of months passed, I went back, and met with the staff again, and they were all happy, thanking me. I said, 'OK, is there anything else?' Six more things went on the flip charts—all facility related. I almost asked, 'When are we going to start talking about the classrooms and the kids?' Instead, I bit my tongue and agreed to meet with them again. We took care of these six things; none of them was major. Tree limbs needed to be trimmed; things like that. I went back. I had the flip charts. 'Any other concerns or things that are holding you back from your work?' No, everything was great, everything was wonderful. 'So there are absolutely no more excuses for why we can't address the improvement of student achievement. We've taken care of all this. And, your sole focus now will be the improvement of student achievement.' In the end, I appointed a new principal and seven teachers left. The new principal and teachers brought new blood into the school, an infusion of ideas and fresh, forward thinking—higher expectations and a renewed sense of caring. The achievement of the school in question improved each subsequent year, but not enough to exit from Program Improvement (see the No Child Left Behind Act of 2001 for accountability standards) status.

"Understanding power is key to effective leadership, and unfortunately, power is abused by some in the field. The negative use of it results in top-down, heavy-handed decision making. There are days when I make some very difficult decisions and I'm the only one who can make them, but power abused is a terrible thing, and I certainly don't feel that a superintendent should abuse it. The converse of abusive power is the power garnered by showing integrity and building trust. It is so important for leaders to do what they say they are going to do. If I say I believe something needs doing, then I'd better do whatever it takes. The easiest way for leaders to lose credibility and to lose trust is to do the opposite of what they say they believe is important.

"In my first administrative position, there was a woman leader of the division for the first time, and she did some things that I have emulated in my years as an administrator. She made sure that each of us wasn't just an expert in our area of responsibility, but that we had multiple experiences. To this day, I credit that experience as important to my professional development. At the other end of the spectrum, I learned what not to do. I was a director at the time. A search consultant, who helped me later, called my supervisor and told him, 'Carmella Franco really needs some fiscal experience. Can you arrange for her to get it?' My supervisor declined, and I had to go outside the district to gain that expertise. It was unfortunate, and showed little concern on his part for mentoring the administrators under his charge. To my mind, he did not carry out an important responsibility—mentoring others.

"What doesn't knock you out will make you a better fighter. For the six years I was in that position as director, I had to be a real scrapper. I dealt with three men who constantly attempted to block everything that I tried to do. I kept asking, particularly in meetings, 'Is there something written in concrete that says we cannot try something new? What about this area? What about doing this?' 'No, that isn't the way we have done it,' they repeatedly responded. I considered it a put-down and just a total lack of respect for a colleague because I was a woman. They had all grown up in the organization, and it made a difference. It's something administrators need to understand. I said, 'After those six years, I could handle anything. I could get through anything.'

"Competence is also key to effective educational leadership at all levels. I believe Latina superintendents today must be totally competent and viewed as knowledgeable and wise. What I try to do is give my administrators—male and female—as many experiences as possible, so that they can grow. For example, I sent my assistant superintendent of human resources to a number of business workshops because he was going to be my point person in our search for a new CBO [chief business officer]. An interim assisted, but I gave him this opportunity. He showed that he could handle it, and the experience helped him grow as an administrator and as a person.

"I also had a Latina director—absolutely as sharp as can be. I sent her to conferences that I thought would benefit her. I gave her a new area to oversee before I left and combined her position with another one so that she had greater authority. She exemplifies competency. She knows her field inside and out. I see her as a future superintendent, and I wanted to provide those steps leading to competency in multiple areas, so that she does well. I did a lot of coaching with her, particularly in staffing and politically tinged situations.

"When I look back over my years in education, I view helping others succeed as a moral imperative. To help them learn how to avoid the pitfalls, to keep their integrity intact, to get through situations as unscathed as they can, and to be better people for it. Particularly, Latinas and other people of color—to open doors for them. I had to force my way through some doors on my way up the ladder. It would have been nice to have had some extra assistance. I did have mentors, but I didn't receive the type of mentoring that I engaged in at Woodland.

"A further challenge for women in educational leadership is related to family. My husband, Thomas Jackson, is an educator. He was a high school principal for fourteen years and has overseen student teachers at the college level for the past eight years. We have no children, but I have three nieces and two nephews. We put our eldest niece through college, so that was a commitment. She earned a degree in marine biology and is now married to a surgeon. The other nieces and nephews are still school age.

"I have been successful in my career, in many ways thanks to my husband. He took on extra responsibilities when I had long days. He had long days, too, so we took turns. But he took the major role. He loves cooking. He has always done it, and I appreciate his willingness and ability to do so. When I was working on my dissertation, he took over all the household chores. I was able to write it in the eight months even though I was in a new job the last two years of the doctorate. I would get home about eight o'clock at night. He'd have a bite for me to eat, and say, 'Get to the table,' and I would write until 1:00 a.m. every weekday, and then twelve and thirteen hours on Saturdays and Sundays.

"In those years, I would have liked to have seen the rest of my family, especially my parents, more often. I didn't get a chance early in my career, so I try to make up for it now when I have time. I struggled with that part of the job. A turning point in my attention to balancing family and work occurred when my niece, who is now ten, was diagnosed with a very aggressive cancer at age two. Doctors had to remove one of her eyes. She recovered and has done wonderfully. That event caused me to change. Afterward I made sure that every weekend, one day was clear for family. It's unfortunate that sometimes there are turning points like these.

"There have been others as well. I knew an assistant superintendent with a two-year-old who was working on her doctorate. She was away from home eight weekends in a row, working on it. I would not recommend that, but that was her choice. Women superintendents my age had a great deal of weight on their shoulders with regard to the job. We have been expected to work double, to do double. The newer breed of superintendent seems to be doing some things differently. I know one new superintendent who, when she was hired, told her board, 'I need to be at home three nights a week, with my family, and home by eight other nights to say good night to my children and to do all the little things to end the day with them.' I admire her for being able to say that. I never said one word to my board when I had a family event. If they said there was an event on a Saturday, and I had something else, I sacrificed my family time. I knew that I couldn't miss the school-related event. Now, people speak up, and I speak up, even in my interim position. It's good that women don't have to make those types of sacrifices as frequently as some of us did in the past. I did, and hopefully I helped lay a foundation for women so that they can insist on family time. It's an interesting time for women leaders, evolving and changing. We may be at a place, or getting to a place, where such action is more acceptable. I don't hear as much about the making of sacrifices."

Carmella Franco—a Latina, an educational leader, a winner—is certainly not afraid to fight for what she believes. She's boxing tough, tried, tested, and found true. But she brings a gentle side to the ring as well. Among the obligatory books about educational leadership lining her bookshelves sits a collection of delicate teacups in various shades of pink and white, which are gifts either from friends or from her two late aunts who also collected them. Each cup carries a special and personal memory of leading, fighting, or winning.

Note: Carmella retired from the Woodland District in 2009. In May 2010, as this book was going to press, she was appointed the Trustee of the Alisal Union School District in the city of Salinas (Monterey County), for a period of at least three years, by the California State Board of Education. As such she is authorized to serve as the Board of the school district, directly supervising the District's Interim Superintendent. She is responsible for rebuilding and restructuring the school district academically to ensure eventual exit from Program Improvement status under the *No Child Left Behind* Act.

BIBLIOGRAPHICAL NOTE

Carmella Franco's story came alive through several interviews, the first of which was conducted by Salwa Zaki in March 2006, with follow-up interviews in November 2008 and September 2009. E-mail exchanges from December 2008 through October 2009 further refined the story. Franco's 2008 curriculum vitae; her 2006 Whittier City School District biography; "WJUSD Names New Leader" from the *Daily Democrat* of July 18, 2008; "Interim Schools Chief for WJUSD" from the *Davis Enterprise* of July 18, 2008; and the Woodland Joint Unified School District Mission Statement added depth and understanding.

SIX

FAITH, FAMILY, AND FORTITUDE—IN A HIGHER EDUCATION JOURNEY

Christine Johnson

"I'VE HEARD IT SAID that the first half of your life is spent finding your gifts, and the second half is spent giving them away. From a young age I yearned to use my time in service to others, to be a blessing to those around me. I am profoundly Catholic and all the fundamentals of me come from my faith. I love people. I care for others. I care about justice. I care a lot about the poor. I want to make a difference and serve others. It's that notion of service to others before self. Over time I refined my ideas and focused the use of my gifts through work I love. I believe my gifts include optimism, intellectual curiosity, self-motivation, compassion, and intuition. My personal mission became to use these gifts to uplift humanity through education. It continues to be a driving force in my life.

"Who I am also comes from my family. My parents contributed to my value system. How you treat others, how you share, how you respect others, and this obligation to do something outside of yourself were continually reinforced throughout my childhood. At the same time I learned strength and independence.

"I grew up in ranch country outside of Hachita in 1953. Hachita is located in the southwestern corner of New Mexico, closer to Tucson, Arizona, than Taos, Albuquerque, or Santa Fe. In its heyday in the early 1800s, the town was home to 775 hearty souls. By the time I came along, fewer than fifty people lived there. Our ranch was an hour away from a community of any appreciable size. Our family had to be self-reliant. We depended on each other for everything, especially companionship.

"Growing up, I went to a little two-room schoolhouse. Both my older brothers, Mike and Jim, and my younger ones, Charlie and David, called me a teacher's pet. And I was the teacher's pet! It's part of our family story. Even my husband, a city boy from Philadelphia, teases me about it. Mrs. Miriam Henke, my first teacher, gave me books to read and my first leadership role in education. I was in charge of the library. It was such a privilege. I loved being in charge of the library.

"At home, the boys worked on the ranch with Dad. I helped around the house. There were no girls to play with. Everyone, including me, rodeoed. My event was barrel racing, but I never excelled like my brothers did. By the time we got to high school, our schoolhouse had closed and we rode a bus an hour each way to school in Lordsburg. I became president of the student body and a member of the National Honor Society once we moved to the new school.

"My background gives me a unique cultural fingerprint— rural, western, Anglo, Hispanic, and Catholic. The combination provides me with wonderful perspective. I grew up in a bilingual, bicultural home. Rosa, my mom, was a native of Mexico and that culture's language, food, and music were important parts of our lives. My dad, Carlos, was Anglo and Mexican. So, we gained an appreciation for a different language and culture from family members and grandparents who wanted us to speak Spanish.

But we also had a fine grasp on mainstream America. I am also from the West and that part of the country has a culture of its own that engenders people who live there with a frontier spirit. We take risks; we work hard; we expect to get something out of our hard work. When your dad is a rancher you do work hard, but you also get a great deal of joy out of it and you grow close as a family because you work as a team.

"Generally, dads tell their daughters how beautiful they are. My dad always told me how smart I was. He told me I was beautiful too. But he always stressed being smart. I have a letter he wrote me when I was ten. I read it every year on my birthday. It's a treasure. It tells me I am beautiful; I am smart; I am a blessing to our family. It's so inspiring, it chokes me up every time I think about it. School was that way too; my teachers pushed and inspired. I wanted them to like me and they did.

"We weren't a family of means, but we didn't know it. We were rich in love and aspiration and service to others. My parents expected us to go to college, but they didn't have the money to send us. So they expected us to get good grades so we could get scholarships. All five of us went to college at New Mexico State University in Las Cruces on scholarships. My brothers studied business. I started out in business, but ended up in education. Later, I went on to earn a master's and a Ph.D. in education administration at the University of Colorado, Boulder. We are all first-generation collegegoers.

"When I think about the person I have become, I owe what I am to what I learned from my family. I grew up to be a strong woman because of my family. My brothers and I are still close. I was especially close to my dad, who died several years ago. My mom, who lived well into her eighties, was a caring role model: a woman of strength and quiet confidence, who was the source of inspiration and courage for our family. She was petite, but so energetic, assertive, and loving.

"I knew I wanted a graduate degree, and early on I knew I wanted to be in a leadership position. My goal was to finish my Ph.D. before I turned thirty, and I did. I commuted to Boulder while teaching English and Spanish at Denver's Thomas Jefferson High School and later as principal of Horace Mann Middle School, also in Denver. I continued to work until I was offered a fellowship that targeted up-and-coming leaders in the Denver Public Schools. I left Horace Mann and spent a year in the program. I felt like I had abandoned a school that needed strong leadership. That's one of the things I feel badly about careerwise, but I believed that an opportunity to complete my doctorate was an opportunity I had to seize.

"In my dissertation, I applied business leadership techniques to the educational setting. My timing was appropriate because Colorado had just initiated a program to train principals to be more effective leaders. After I graduated I became principal at Lincoln High School, where I gained national attention and was named Colorado Principal of the Year in 1989. As part of winning that award, I traveled to Washington, D.C. My trip to the nation's capital was the beginning of a long relationship with federal education policy makers. In 1990, then U.S. Secretary of Education Lauro Cavazos asked me to serve on the National Assessment Governing Board. There I served on a twenty-member commission that examined the future of twelfth grade assessment instruments. Lamar Alexander continued my appointment so that I could work on the Nation's Report Card, which set academic standards and achievement levels for students. Later, I was part of a group of U.S. college presidents and chancellors that the Department of Education assembled to examine and redefine the mission of American community colleges.

"In Colorado I left Lincoln High School to become assistant superintendent of the Littleton School District, and the governor appointed me to the Colorado Commission for Higher Education, where I served eight years, three as the commission's chair. In 1993, I began serving as the director of Urban Initiatives with the Education Commission of the States [ECS]. We provided policy development, analysis, and implementation assistance on matters concerning accountability, standards and assessment, capital development, finance, governance, urban education, and innovation of all kinds at all levels, such as [the] charter school movement that began in the '90s as part of parental choice.

"In 1998, I became chief academic officer for the Community Colleges of Colorado. I provided academic leadership and direction for the state's largest higher education system, which includes thirteen system colleges, two local district colleges, the Higher Education Advanced Technology Center, and Colorado Community Colleges Online. I led workforce development and innovation efforts and built statewide strategic partnerships with all industry sectors. Under my direction, linkages with public schools across the state resulted in new articulation and 2 + 2 efforts that improved student access across the education sectors.

"Locally, we suffer from what is known as the Colorado Paradox. Our state ranks near the top in the number of residents who hold at least a bachelor's degree, but at the same time, it lags all but three states in sending our own high school students to college. For many teens growing up in Denver in particular, college is an unknown because their parents are not college graduates. Too many of them can't imagine themselves as college students. Financial barriers are major obstacles, but the economic reality is that without a degree, they will earn less money and be less competitive in today's marketplace.

"My heart has always been with urban students and advancing urban education. When Byron McClenney left the Community College of Denver (CCD) in 2000, I thought, 'That is the college I want to lead.' I served as CCD's president for six years. I was Colorado's first Latina college president.

"When I took over CCD, we expected people to seek us out. I decided to emphasize the community and reach out to them. Our goal became to provide whatever support students needed to stay in college, earn a degree, transfer to a four-year institution, or get a good job, including holding their hands while making them accountable for their education.

"I relied on my long-term relationship with Denver Public Schools to establish partnerships that brought their students to CCD. We developed a partnership with Emily Griffith Opportunity School that streamlined similar programs at both schools and started their students on a path that could lead well beyond an associate's degree. We helped develop the Middle College of Denver High School. There, students work on their high school diplomas and associate degrees concurrently.

"In the early 2000s, Colorado's need for nurses and other health care workers reached crisis level. In response to the high demand, we initiated community and business partnerships that put more nurses into the workforce. One such program, HealthOne (named for the program's sponsor, Denver's largest health-care provider), offered a full-tuition scholarship to nursing students who agreed to work for the company after graduation. In another, the University of Phoenix provided scholarships to graduate-level nursing students that were contingent on them teaching in CCD's nursing program. Several long-term-care facilities established CCD programs that trained certified nurse's aides to become licensed practical nurses. Those who graduated could continue at CCD to earn associate's degrees in nursing and become registered nurses."

During her tenure as president, Johnson led the college to national prominence and did so during Colorado's most dramatic state funding cuts in history alongside rapid enrollment growth. From 2001 to 2007, CCD was the second-fastest-growing community college nationwide. Enrollment in 2002–03 alone rose about 20 percent, the most of any public college or university in Colorado. Simultaneously, state support for the college went from 60 percent to 25 percent. When she took office, Johnson and her leadership team brought the college out of a $1 million deficit and built a modest reserve, while statewide higher education suffered further major budget cuts. For CCD it meant 15 percent [in] state cuts annually for three consecutive years. At a peak growth period, state community colleges suffered a 17 percent reversion in state funding on top of a 10.6 percent reversion the year before.

"At the same time, we were recognized by the Colorado General Assembly as a College of Excellence for our high student success and retention, workforce innovation in meeting business and industry needs, and for administrative efficiency. The college earned recognition for four consecutive years as a Workforce Innovator by the U.S. Department of Labor for its workplace learning program and responsiveness to high industry demands. The North Carolina Center for Public Policy Research ranked CCD among the top thirteen (two- and four-year) higher education institutions in the country for high student success and retention in the first year of college. The center's director called CCD the 'gold standard in the community college world.'

"MetLife Foundation chose CCD as one of the 'four best practices' colleges in the country. And the college was featured in a PBS documentary called *Learning Matters* about the state of

America's higher education. The yearlong filming project examined teaching and learning in four different types of higher education institutions—a highly selective private institution (Amherst), a big public four-year (Arizona State), a smaller four-year (Western Kentucky), and one community college (Community College of Denver).

"Students keep you grounded. They're that daily reminder of why we're here. CCD is classified as a Hispanic-Serving Institution with almost 30 percent of its students carrying that identifier. When I was at CCD, we served the most diverse student population of any college or university in Colorado with almost 60 percent of our students coming from underrepresented groups. We became the leading point of access to higher education for first-time college enrollees from the city and county of Denver. In any given year first-generation students make up about 65 percent of CCD's more than 13,000 students.

"Many families don't believe it is financially possible for their children to go to college. Their children help support their families and the families need the money. When you don't have food or might get evicted, the rent takes priority over college tuition. Newer immigrants can also feel insecure about college. There's a confidence barrier, a lack of tradition. We didn't just give them a financial aid form—we helped them fill it out. We demystified the paperwork. There was a lot of hand-holding. We called it *purposeful hand-holding*. My second year as president, the retention rate for students in the first-generation programs was a remarkably high 84 percent. Frank Newman, who headed ECS for years and was key in the Futures Project at Brown University, noted, 'What Denver has done that is more effective than others is reaching out to these students.'

"One of our most successful first-generation programs, which started prior to my presidency but continued to strengthen during my years at CCD, was the Access and Success Project. Although not all first-generation collegegoers needed or wanted to participate in this program, support services were available to all.

"Educational case management teams of case managers, program coordinators, faculty, and student ambassadors formed the backbone of the program. Through them we provided holistic advising, career planning, and academic retention strategies, including advanced computer training, bilingual support groups, laboratory study groups, one-to-one tutoring, mandatory remediation in mathematics and English, and supplemental instruction. The term used was *intrusive advising.* Each case manager handled three hundred students, and one of their duties was to advocate for students in ways that helped them overcome culture barriers. For instance, if someone's grandparent dies in Mexico, the student needs to be gone for two weeks in order to pay proper respect. In a traditional system if you miss two weeks you are gone. So, we talked to faculty to help the student work things out. We also continued to mentor and tutor in the second year when students moved into major courses because they often suffered an academic culture shock.

"During my time at CCD, I started my day at 5 a.m. and finished up around 8 p.m. Today, my workday is more varied. I begin each day with prayer and scripture reading and then exercise. Mostly I use the NordicTrack. But I love being outdoors, so I prefer a quick walk around the neighborhood, maybe half an hour. We live in the foothills, so it's good aerobic exercise. I eat well, I'm not a junk-food lover, but I definitely like pastry and chocolate. My husband of twenty years and I stay physically active. Carl [Griffin], that's his name, is a retired IBM executive, so he has time and I make time. We fish, we hike, we cross-country ski, we snowshoe.

"I have been blessed with good health, optimism, energy, and joy in living. I make time and enjoy time in all areas of life: spiritual, familial, professional, community. I believe balance and fulfillment in these areas give me energy and resilience. I am also fueled by quiet time in the mountains or any other natural setting. Time alone in nature is truly an extraordinary way to stay grounded, healthy, and optimistic. My daily time alone both calms and exhilarates me.

"I am upbeat. I don't get down. I am an eternal optimist. When I get up I am ready to go and always in a great mood. I really don't get stressed. If I count on someone to do something and it doesn't get done, it doesn't stress me, it disappoints me. I say to that person, 'I trusted you to do x and y and you didn't. I don't own your responsibility, you do.' In my midyear reviews I liked to build people up. I wanted them to see all the good they were doing, but I also gave very honest feedback because that's how we grow. I wouldn't say, 'Oh, you blew it,' but rather, 'How do you think you are doing in this area?' and then follow up with 'How might you improve?'

"I believe good things will happen. I have this enormous reservoir of energy. My faith lifts me up. I work hard. I get physically tired and that's okay because I know that I am doing something to make life better for students or the community every day. Carl and I have no children of our own. We do enjoy over a dozen nieces and nephews and their children. But in truth, my work and my students have been my surrogate children.

"I live my life with integrity and gusto. How I choose to use my energy signals my passion and identifies my priorities. I am energized by work in education. It is my calling, my life's work.

There is so much to be done, and no time, no person, no energy to waste. I understand that I can't expect other people to get up early, work all day, and do it again the next day. Not everyone has my level of energy. I had to remember when I was at CCD that if I had an employee with a young family, going to every college activity and being seen was not as important as being with that child.

"Passion, however, is what distinguishes people who are average from people who are excellent because it suggests a depth of caring. I have heard of companies that hire using only two criteria, passion and attitude. In the past, when I interviewed potential employees, I told them I was interviewing them for their hearts. I already knew they were competent. What I wanted to know about was their commitment. I wanted to see in them a belief in endless opportunities.

"I am a total extrovert. I love people and intuitively know when they are with me or not. I have great empathy for others and that makes me more responsive to them. I connect with people easily. I engage in artful listening—really hearing what people want to know so that I can respond to their concerns. I think human beings are interesting. I am curious about their life experience, culture, language, religion. I am a student of people and have enormous respect for humanity.

"I've worked very hard all of my life. My dad used to talk about honor and believed that you honored your word and other people. And we had family honor. We were never to do anything to shame our family or lose honor. Those ideas stayed with me and have come to mean personal integrity. It's about being trustworthy. Language and words are powerful tools and we can use them to do good or bad. All I have is my credibility. I'm only as good as what I say I will do and then do."

In 2002 Mexican President Vicente Fox named Christine and fifty-two other Americans of Hispanic heritage Women of Distinction. Christine told the *Denver Post* that President Fox believed she and the others were good role models for women in Mexico. She was a member of two trade missions to Mexico. She's been called on by five U.S. secretaries of education (Laura Cavazos, Lamar Alexander, Richard Riley, Rod Paige, and Margaret Spellings) to influence national policy discussions through service on national boards, commissions, task forces, and work groups. She has served on the boards of the Hispanic Association of Colleges and Universities, National Community College Hispanic Council, American Council on Education Minorities in Higher Education Commission, College Board National Commission on Community Colleges, State Scholars Initiative Advisory Board, and the Lumina Foundation Policy Advisory Board. She received numerous awards and honors including the Girl Scouts of America's Young Women of Distinction Award.

In June 2007 Nancy McCallin, president of the Colorado Community College System, fired Christine Johnson.

When McCallin took over in 2004, the state mandated that the system slash spending and create a centralized computer system. In response, she inaugurated an era of centralized power, financial audits, and close supervision of once independent presidents. McCallin required college presidents to sign a loyalty oath, which stated that the community college presidents' primary responsibility was to the system president and its board. The intended purpose of the oath was system unification. Instead, administrators suggested that it resulted in a climate of fear where disagreement was treated as insubordination. The $25 million centralized computer system came online in 2004. But in 2007 it consistently mishandled payments, produced inaccurate financial reports, and failed to register thousands of students. Even so McCallin's board chair described her as phenomenal.

An anonymous tip from a former CCD employee raised concerns about an Iranian instructor, who had developed courses for students located in Middle Eastern countries, because he was paid three times more than other CCD instructors. McCallin ordered an investigation that generated three allegations against Johnson: one about the Iranian instructor suggesting that Johnson let him establish health and education programs in the United Arab Emirates without the required permission from McCallin and that Johnson approved paying him student recruiting fees; another alleged that she directed the college's chief financial officer (CFO) to misrepresent the amount held by the college in its reserve account; and the third accused her of failing to ensure that proper student records were on file, potentially allowing illegal immigrants to attend college.

In the first instance, CCD was not the first Colorado public college to hire the Iranian instructor. He had worked for five other two- and four-year institutions prior to joining CCD's faculty and had been an instructor at CCD prior to Johnson's presidency. He started at Colorado State University-Pueblo in 1981. By 1985 he was at Pikes Peak Community College, where he developed his signature program consisting of three- to eight-week intensive courses taught off campus or online to students located primarily in the Middle East. One of his previous employers even paid to fly him to Dubai and Iran, where he explored international education programs, recruited students, and dined with United Arab Emirates dignitaries. By the time he started at CCD he'd been working in Colorado higher education institutions for twenty years.

In the second case, problems with the computer system's faulty financial reporting were rampant. At CCD one CFO was forced to quit because she felt she was flying blind and didn't have the tools she needed to do her job. The new CFO believed the college had more reserves than were required but was reluctant to report it for fear that either her figures were inaccurate and she had overstated the amount on hand or they were correct and reversions similar to those in the college's recent past might be required. The decision made was to say that Johnson and the CFO didn't know how to calculate the reserve amount. A board representative said the board would never ask a college to give money back but admitted that the computer system had major problems. State officials added that the calculation process was complicated and confusing.

Regarding the third accusation, speculation surfaced about whether Johnson's advocacy on behalf of undocumented students, typically children brought into the country illegally by family members seeking work, might have gotten her in trouble. Such individuals are not barred from attending school but can do so only on nonresident status and are not entitled to federal financial aid. Johnson went out and raised private money to assist those students.

Hundreds of e-mail exchanges obtained by the *Rocky Mountain News* suggest that McCallin and Johnson clashed for months before the final showdown and depict, at best, a strained relationship between the two prior to Johnson's public ouster. After the charges were made, Johnson disputed the claims and pointed to her track record of previous clean audits. A preliminary audit failed to uncover any record of money that had been misspent but did find that adequate protections were not in place to guard against the problems highlighted in the allegations made against her. The subsequent state audit ordered by McCallin did not support the original allegations made concerning Johnson's conduct as president.

Presidents are at-will employees who can be terminated anytime with or without cause. And during the first three years of

McCallin's tenure, nine of thirteen presidents either left, retired, or were fired. Several prominent community members believed that Johnson was treated too harshly, that the system dumped an excellent leader. To them, it seemed that the situation could have been remedied through the audit process in which a state legislative audit committee provides opportunities for institutions to correct their errors annually. In Johnson's case, no opportunity was given to work things out. The Hispanic community viewed her dismissal as a great loss. Her discharge sent a chill throughout the system. In October 2008 Johnson and the system reached an "amicable" settlement in which she agreed not to sue the system, the system paid her attorney's fees, and it appears that some remuneration was paid to Johnson.

"In reaching a settlement agreement with the Colorado Community College System, I agreed to not speak about my dismissal, and I have not and will not. I've had the privilege of serving in numerous leadership roles in Colorado and have worked with outstanding professionals for over thirty years. There are few people who can say they have loved their work every day, and I can honestly say that I have. I am proud of all the work accomplished on behalf of students in every role I had. I am particularly fortunate to have remained in Colorado all these years to see the fruits of my work in student and employee success and their continued upward movement.

"I've always believed that human nature is full of goodness and potential. Ernie Boyer once said, 'It is as natural to help as it is to hurt.' I believe this. In leadership roles I've held, I've sought the best in others to tap undiscovered gifts, to encourage with a word or with added responsibility, to edify, and to strengthen. At CCD, it was easy to find ways to encourage and build others, as the work was so deeply meaningful and impactful. I loved CCD and its mission, the students and communities it served, the college's character and ethos. People at CCD literally changed lives every day, inspired by students and the challenges they overcame. CCD was a place where individuals and the organization worked to realize full potential. The college and its mission, students, and communities will always hold a special place in my heart.

"One of our greatest gifts is time and the use of time, so I've been disciplined about making my time count—using it well, using it to do good, using it to be a person worth emulating. I've taken numerous risks professionally, stood on principle, and spoken out when others would not. One of the greatest professional challenges I experienced was dismissal from an institution I loved and had dedicated my heart and soul to serving. It was a painful and unexpected experience. But I was determined to not have the dismissal define me or change my outlook and optimism. I worked at learning more about myself, about human nature, about organizations. My deep faith gave me strength, perseverance, and courage. Unfortunate and unexpected things happen in life to test our character, our capacity for love, our clarity of purpose. It isn't the trial itself that tests us, but who we choose to be at the other end. I know that this test has made me stronger, more determined, more purposeful.

"When I think about me as a person, I find that I've learned that I have both strengths and weaknesses. I trust people, and on occasion I trusted individuals who were not trustworthy. I speak out when I see inequities; I ask questions; I seek answers. I give voice to others. Perhaps these actions were not valued and I missed the cues. I could have stayed silent, but I'm unable to look the other way when things aren't right. And I am willing to pay the price for speaking out. It's a matter of personal integrity and principle to me. I have come to the realization that sometimes in losing, we win, and that in winning we can lose. Life is full of challenges and opportunities, and growth is accelerated in the toughest moments and the greatest struggles.

"Today, I know that I am whole at the core of my being, intrinsically the same person with the same values and outlook, a little wiser, a little humbler, a lot more courageous, and a lot more grateful. The storm is past, the sky is blue, and there is a whole world of need that deserves my full commitment, dedication, and passion.

"I ended up at the University of Colorado (UC) Denver through an invitation Chancellor Roy Wilson made to me the day after I was dismissed. He asked me to join UC Denver, saying, 'The university can use you.' I was in shock that day, but over six months later I called to find out if he meant what he said. I was delighted to join a superb leadership team where I work primarily with the Community College Leadership and Policy Center (CCLPC) and Latino Policy and Research Center (LPRC).

"I am actively involved in the fund-raising and program development phases of the CCLPC. The LPRC has been a part of UC Denver for a decade. My role is to build on its prior work and to expand its research and policy agenda to broader topics that impact the Latino community, for instance, education, criminal justice, and immigration, as well as to sustain its health care focus. Rebuilding the university's outreach and service to the Latino community of Colorado is vital.

"When I see the staggering human, social, and economic costs of an undereducated individual multiplied by the communities, families, and countries touched by this crisis, I am motivated to do all that I can to impact that one more person, family, community, and our country. I am confident the next several decades of my work will unfold in interesting and unpredictable ways. I believe I will work in new ways with new partners to address the moral imperative we face. I hope my future work impacts the nation and indeed people across the world. It is time for new beginnings and new ventures—and I am prepared for the opportunities and challenges that lie ahead. I am eager to focus on the future."

In August 2010, Christine Johnson accepted her next new beginning by becoming the Chancellor of the Community Colleges of Spokane, Washington.

BIBLIOGRAPHICAL NOTE

Christine Johnson's story came alive through several interviews, the first of which was conducted by Adrienne Hyle in January 2007. Follow-up interviews were conducted in August and September 2009. In addition, e-mail exchanges; Johnson's 2008 résumé; a December 2004 interview with *Hispanic Outlook*; a 2001 press release from the Office of the Mayor of Denver about a national award for the community college's workforce program; her CCD president's profile and 2007 list of achievements; and "A Helping Hand: The Community College of Denver Reaches Out to First-Generation Students" in 2004 in *Crosstalk*, *12*(1), 4–5, by Kay Mills added depth and understanding.

The material about Johnson's dismissal came from the following articles in the *Rocky Mountain News*: "Hispanic leaders seek answers for dismissal of CCD president," by Nancy Mitchell, July 1, 2007; "A college president is gone: How it happened," by Katie Kerwin McCrimmon, September 25, 2007; "OK of prof's work contributes to college chief losing her job," by Jeff Kass, September 26, 2007; "Head of community colleges: Ouster was 'not a witch hunt'" by Katie Kerwin McCrimmon, September 27, 2007; "Colorado Community College System, fired president reach deal," by Katie Kerwin McCrimmon, November 20, 2008 and from the following articles in the *Denver Post*: "CCD chief dismissal amid audit," by Mark P. Couch, June 19, 2007; "Audit spurs college leader's firing" by Mark P. Couch and Elizabeth Aguilera, June 20, 2007; "Deceit felled college chief" by Allison Sherry and Elizabeth Aguilera, June 21, 2007. An October 31, 2008, press release from the Colorado Community College System also provided information.

seven

INVEST IN YOUR LIFE FULLY—WITHOUT FEAR

Thelma López-Lira

"I AM A FIFTY-ONE-YEAR-OLD PROFESSIONAL, mother, and wife who struggles through life the best way she can. People say I am nice and that I get along with everybody. I am tolerant; I only argue if I think the dispute is worth it. I don't try to change people who don't want to change. I don't try to give people answers to questions they don't want answered. I accept people the way they are.

"And, I live my life the way I want. People can have opinions about my life, but they don't infringe on it, except for family; they are the only ones to whom I've given that power. Having a family was the best personal decision I ever made. My children have more influence on me than my husband does. Even so, I am aware that I must be true to myself before I follow their desires. I am a doctor (M.D.) and I am passionate about my patients. My children know this. They have learned that Mom has to work, and if they need something from me they often have to wait. If they have a meeting or a conference they want me to attend, then they have learned to tell me with enough lead time so I can make arrangements in my schedule. I don't have the luxury of doing things on the spur of the moment. I cannot be there for them 'right now.' My children are very good at postponing gratification. They have made many sacrifices for my career.

"I was born in Monterrey, Nuevo León, México. I never knew my paternal grandparents. The only grandparent I remember is my *abuela* on my mother's side. She was a strict woman who worked hard. By the time we were ready to go to school in the morning she had already finished cleaning the house. I remember jumping over the mop on my way out the door. Those were hard years. She was a woman who gave everything to us. Later when she became ill, I helped take care of her.

"My mother is like my grandma. She has always been strict and hardworking. We inherited our strong work ethic from her. Even now, she has great stamina and extreme determination. I don't know of any other eighty-year-old woman who has a job as an office manager. When she was seventy years old she decided to go into an assisted-living facility. She visited places until she found one she was comfortable with. I admire that, the ability to meet one's own needs so that others don't have to meet them for you.

"I didn't know my father well. I really only have two memories of him, one good and one bad. The good memory took place when he came to the house to talk with Mom and I ran to him. He grabbed me and carried me. I was able to reach the top of the door frame. I felt so tall, so unique. I was in heaven at that moment. I was three, yet I remember it like it was yesterday. Eventually my parents divorced, and I didn't see him again until I was in medical school. One day he ended up at my sister's house when I was visiting her. He didn't remember my name. He called me by a different name. He did not remember Thelma, his own daughter. It was sad.

"My formative years were shaped in part by my mother and grandmother. But the greatest impact in my life came from my four siblings. I am the youngest one. Mom worked outside of the home, first as a secretary and later in management positions, to support us. She has always been an extremely dedicated person who made sure that we succeeded. That was her goal in life, and she is proud of what we have accomplished. But much of the mothering I received came from my sisters and brother, out of necessity, not by choice.

"The oldest of my four siblings is five years older than I am. She works as a consultant in Monterrey, México. She has been in private practice for the last thirty-five years. She has a bachelor's degree in psychology and a master's degree in organizational psychology from the Universidad de Monterrey. My second oldest sister is one year younger than the oldest. She works in education and as a consultant and writer and lives in the U.S. like I do. She has a bachelor's degree in psychology from the Universidad de Monterrey and a master's degree in psychoanalytic psychotherapy from the Instituto de Psicoterapia in San Pedro Garza García, México. She also has a Ph.D. in counselor education and supervision from Syracuse University in New York. Our brother is two years older than I am. He teaches at the Instituto Tecnológico de Monterrey. He has a bachelor's degree in mechanical engineering from the Instituto Tecnológico de Monterrey and a master's degree in metallurgy from the Massachusetts Institute of Technology in Boston. My other sister is one year older than I. She has bachelor's and master's degrees from the Universidad de Monterrey in adult education. She heads programs in postgraduate education in the area of safety in Monterrey. We are like stair steps—one right after the other.

"I have a medical degree from the Universidad Autónoma de Nuevo León in Monterrey, board certification in psychiatry from

the University of Houston, and another residency and board certification in child psychiatry. I also did two years of postgraduate
psychoanalytic training in Galveston, Texas. My husband is a doctor with a degree from Universidad Autónoma de Nuevo León
and board certification in obstetrics and gynecology from the
University of Houston. We have been in private practice for fifteen years in Corpus Christi.

"We have two children. The oldest, Brenda, is in eleventh
grade at Incarnate Word High School. She is good in class and
loves books. She is self-disciplined. I admire her ability to set her
goals and stick to them. She reminds me of me at her age. She is
true to herself and well adjusted but not particularly sociable—a
few good friends, that's all she seems to need.

"Our son, Kevin, is fourteen. He has attention-deficit-hyperac-
tivity disorder (ADHD). He is extremely smart, with a 140 IQ.
But even simple tasks can overwhelm him and this works against
him. He's a great kid, a sweet guy, and a good brother. I worry
about him. He has been struggling, and we try to give him as
much positive reinforcement as possible. We know he can be
successful because my husband has ADHD. It was hard for him
to overcome it, but he did. Our awareness of the situation makes
it somewhat easier for Kevin than it was for his dad.

"When Brenda turned sixteen in 2009, we gave her a car. I
told her that we were celebrating my independence, not just her
birthday! Having an extra driver in the house works well for me.
I used to wake up at 4:45 each morning so that I could get them
to swimming classes. I dropped them off by 6:15 and started my
hospital rounds. Now I can wake up at 6:15, say good-bye to them,
and get ready to start my day, usually by eight. It takes me all
morning to do rounds at two hospitals. By then, my first patient
is waiting at the office. I see patients until around 5:30 and follow
up with about an hour's worth of paperwork. If I have patients to

see in the hospital I go back and see them. Sometimes I don't get finished until eight at night. I don't like that because it gives me only a couple of hours with the family before bedtime. I prefer to get home by six, cook dinner, and sit down to a meal together.

"Every third weekend I am on call. I see somewhere between thirty-five and forty-five patients each of those days, so my entire weekend is pretty much shot. I am very committed to my patients. I derive great satisfaction and energy from working with them. I can be tired but when patients come into my office I get energized and attuned to them. I have to fully understand their psychiatric needs because if I don't I might prescribe a treatment that will not work. If I start losing energy I give myself a few minutes of fantasizing about how good my last vacation was and how great my next one will be. Doing so allows me to recharge. This type of work takes stamina.

"I love what I do. I am proud of what I do. I try to take care of my patients the best way possible. I am meticulous. I don't skip steps. For example, most psychiatrists do not order general laboratory work for their patients. They believe that the family doctor will do it. I ask my patients if their family doctor will do it and ask to see the lab work results in order to assess their complete physical state. If their family doctor does not order the lab work once a year, then I do it. I have discovered cancer, juvenile diabetes, and other conditions that have nothing to do with psychiatry because I am so thorough. When I do [discover something] I send them to a medical specialist.

"I always wanted to have a small practice, but Corpus Christi doesn't have enough psychiatrists, and I am the only Hispanic female psychiatrist. Today, I have more patients than I can handle. I am not taking new patients. I never thought that I would have such a large practice.

"My patients depend on me to help them look for answers to their problems. It is easy to pretend that we know it all when the truth is we don't. I know I am competent. But I also must be self-assured enough to say to a patient, 'I don't know just yet. But I am willing to work with you until we figure it out.' Good communication is key.

"I must be able to explain to my patients what is going on with them. They must trust me. I often think of myself as a teacher more than a doctor. I teach my patients on a daily basis. I talk to my patients about multiple variables, either of their illness or their treatment. We discuss what they can expect with their treatment and what changes they might need to make in their lifestyle. I tell them why. For instance, antipsychotics are great, but the biggest side effect is that you can gain ten to fifteen pounds per year. If I tell them, 'I am sorry, you are not going to be psychotic but you are going to be fat and you are going to have high blood pressure and diabetes,' then the treatment I am prescribing is really not a very good treatment. I have to convince them that this is the right treatment and that they are going to have to exercise and eat right. It is what their brain needs but at the same time they have to stay in control of these side effects. It's communication at the highest level.

"Occasionally, being bilingual helps with my patients. But typically I only have ten Spanish-speaking patients at any given time. Most of my Anglo patients are fine with our differences and respect them. I am credible. In some instances, however, being bilingual can be a disadvantage. The husband of one of my patients was uncomfortable with me being Hispanic. He fired me. Sometimes I can sense discomfort. There were two older White women. They respected my treatment and followed my recommendations. But I could tell they would not want me as a friend. It seemed like it had to do with me being Hispanic.

"I don't necessarily think that we have to understand all cultures because that would be impossible, but we need to realize that there are differences in this world. People do things differently. I can't change people's culture. I have to work with it. For example, I don't agree with the behavior of many Hispanic individuals and what they value. Corpus Christi has one of the highest rates of teenage pregnancy in the nation. (Nueces County, in which Corpus Christi is located, ranks second highest in teenage pregnancies in the country. Eighty-three percent of Texas teen mothers are Hispanic. Corpus Christi is about 60 percent Hispanic; 30 percent of the city's total population is under the age of 18.) Hispanic individuals here tend to be okay with it. I have had very young patients who have had extreme sexual experiences and abortions. And while my own views do not align with theirs, I have to understand that engaging in sexual activity and becoming pregnant is the way these particular teenagers value themselves. It is not about fighting what they are doing but about understanding why they are in my office. What brought them here? And then work with that. I have to be very focused on the patient's current problem and yet I need to see the whole picture: his or her whole life and how the symptoms and problems fit together.

"I love my job. I definitely am not willing to give up working; this is not an option for me. I think that working keeps me mentally healthy. Having said that, I realize my career cuts into my mothering and parenting. I could work 24/7 if I wanted to. I could work day and night. But I can't. It is impossible. It is not healthy for me as a person, and it is unhealthy for my family. I do try to save as much time as I can for my family. I am willing to postpone certain parts of my own development in the [interest] of my children's development. They come first.

"I have been offered directorships in hospitals, and I have declined. I am not willing to give what it takes, more time, more effort. I tell them, 'The day I am ready to give you what you want me to give you, I will.' Not too long ago, they asked me as a favor to substitute for a director of one of the departments at the hospital. I said yes—but just for a few days because I am reaching my level of inefficiency and I don't like it. I like to be efficient. I like to know that what I am doing I am doing 100 percent. I am not willing to take on responsibilities if [it] means that I will be unable to meet my personal priorities; that would be disingenuous. I need to be able to do what I say I will do and do it with integrity.

"I have integrity and this makes me credible. People trust me and over time that leads to personal power. The power that I have lets me decide what I do and what I don't do. No one else makes those decisions for me in either my professional or personal life. Of course my professional life impacts my personal life. I keep my own power very close to me. I never give power to others about my own development or about my own work. This of course makes me kind of a loner. In the future the situation might change. But today I need to have power over my own destiny. I haven't always thought this way. As a woman I was socialized to take care of others and satisfy their needs. For example, when my husband and I were in medical school, I waited for him to take the lead. I did not want to surpass him. I wanted him to finish before I did. I wanted him to get into a residency and succeed. So I held back until I discovered that I was giving away my power.

"The worst mistake I made was postponing my own goals in the name of 'a relationship.' I think this is the greatest danger for women. I thought of my career as secondary within my household. I did not try to fail but I didn't try to succeed either. I waited for my partner to succeed so that I could start investing in myself. I think now this was the wrong tactic to take, and I don't do it anymore. I do believe in taking care of my children, but I don't believe in taking care of my partner in that way. Coming to that decision has been a long process. At times it has been difficult and I have stumbled. But I have discovered what works best for me. As a woman—I have to take care of myself and my own development and not expect my partner to take care of it for me. Professionally the best decision I ever made was to stop being an old-fashioned woman waiting for my husband to succeed before me.

"My husband and I share offices. However, we have very clear boundaries as to how much we can intrude into each other's work. We don't do it. He can come into my office and ask me about what to do with one of his obstetric patients because he is an obstetrician. This patient might have both an obstetric and a psychiatric issue. I am happy to consult with him. We can consult as we pass each other in the hallway. I might ask him about some urinary tract infection that one of my psychiatric patients has. However, we have absolutely no power over each other's patients. Our offices work independently. Although we own and work in the same building, we have separate staff. We hug each other and we might talk about the house or children. He might bring me lunch. But, all we know about each other's work is perhaps how many patients we have left to see on a particular day. Over time we have grown; we have learned to respect each other's territory. We are there to support each other, but that is all. We are one of the most fluid couples I know. Only professionally do we have this separation. At home we are one and the same.

"There's not a right or wrong way to be a woman. I do believe that many women are in a transition period. We have double or triple responsibilities and we postpone our own personal development for the sake of our families. We have to work harder than men. People expect women to perform less well than men and to be in second place professionally because we often have to put our families first. Truly, if one of my kids gets sick, who is going to miss work? I have that reality in my life, but I also have the flexibility that allows me to do it. Not all women do. The greatest enemy for women is that we allow our partners to dictate our lives. Until we can exercise control over what we do, we will remain in transition.

"When I started medical school I didn't think about being successful. Even today if you ask me if I am successful I will say, 'Well, I do what I want. I guess I am successful.' I firmly believe that whatever it is that you want to do, you should go for it! Set your own goals. Be true to yourself. Have integrity. Invest in your life fully, without fear."

BIBLIOGRAPHICAL NOTE

The story of Thelma López-Lira evolved from a series of three face-to-face interviews and from the personal knowledge of her sister who is one of the authors of this book.

eight

CULTURE DRIVES WHO I AM

Darline Robles

"I LOVE THE WORD *PASSIONATE*. It speaks to the core of any leader's role. If you're not passionate about what the organization stands for, then you're going to be just a caretaker. I look for the hidden strengths in individuals, tap the human potential, and I'm willing to take the hard knocks and punches necessary to deal with the tough problems. I'm not going to settle for less than the best. Taped to the monitor on my computer is a saying by Emma Goodman that I read every day to remind me about why I do what I do: 'No one has yet realized the wealth of sympathy, the kindness and generosity hidden in the soul of a child. The effect of every true education should be to unlock that treasure.' Every day, a teacher, an administrator, or a staff member has a new opportunity to unlock that treasure. How lucky and fortunate for us that we chose this profession!

"I entered the field of public education as a Teacher Corps intern in 1972 in Los Padrinos Juvenile Hall Court School in Los Angeles. I moved on to Montebello Unified School District, where I started as a middle school ESL [English as a second language] teacher, and then into central office administration as a bilingual district coordinator. After serving as both an elementary

and middle school principal, I became an assistant superintendent and then superintendent for four years. From 1995 to 2002,
I worked for the Salt Lake City School District. After seven years
in Salt Lake City I moved back to California, where I am the
executive officer for the Los Angeles County Office of Education
(LACOE), the nation's largest regional education service agency.
The agency assists eighty-one K–12 school districts that educate
1.7 million students. After more than thirty-five years, I am still
passionate about public education.

"I left Montebello because my board at that time made a decision that I couldn't ethically support. One Latino board member
said to me that he didn't think I'd leave. He believed that because
I am Latina, I would never leave my family—or community, for
that matter. I said, 'I can't stay in an environment where I can't
support the decisions being made.' It was the first time in a long
time where someone actually believed that just because I am Latina I didn't have choices—that I would just stay put. That was a
surprise for me. I think if I had not been Latina, if I had been
male or if I had been White, no one would have had those
thoughts. Because I did move, and moved to an area where I
didn't know anyone, it shocked a great number of people. The
fact that my husband and family supported my decision was an
even greater surprise.

"I learned a good lesson in Montebello, though—many Latino
parents are more courageous than I am. We had increasing num-
bers of immigrants, many of whom had struggled to get there. I
met parents who came from El Salvador underneath a bus to get
across the border to the United States. They left their families for
a better life, none of them having jobs, not knowing where they
were going to live, not understanding the customs or the language. I asked the group at my going-away party, 'Why do people
think I'm afraid to move out of state? I'm a citizen. I speak the

language. I can come back home. I have a lot more that I can rely and fall back on than the parents that I'm interacting with every day. How courageous they are!'

"My culture emphasizes family values, cultural understanding of people and relating to them, and accepting people who might be different. It drives many of my actions. My experiences shaped my life as a young girl and my work as a teacher. I grew up in a Mexican American family. I was born in the United States. My parents were born here, and my grandparents on one side were born here. But one of my grandmothers was a Mexican national when she married my grandfather. They had met on the California border in an area called Mexicali and she left her family to join my grandfather in the States. She moved here but never gave up her Mexican citizenship. She felt strongly about her culture and her roots and instilled that sentiment in my cousins and brother and me. We're proud of our Mexican ancestry and also proud to be American. We spent my youth going to Mexicali to be with my family from Mexico. From the day I was born, I've always identified myself as bicultural and Mexican American.

"I grew up in an environment of strong matriarchs. My mother was a working, single parent, and we moved around in search of better schools. In the fifties, most kids stayed within one community, but by the time I was in fourth grade, I'd been in several different schools. My experience in school was a positive one most of the time because I was an early reader, and I didn't have difficulty in school. But even though I stood out as a good student, there wasn't a teacher who ever acknowledged that I was new to that school. I realized early on that kids from cultures different from the mainstream might not get the best advantages and opportunities.

"Mom raised two children through very difficult times. There were always child care issues. Yet we knew we were her number one priority. She taught us, through her actions, how to care for, trust, and respect each other, and every day she demonstrated her unconditional love. She taught me how to read and to think independently. She instilled in me confidence, self-esteem, and the belief that I could do and be whatever I desired despite our circumstances. She saw only the good in me, in my heart and soul, and unlocked that treasure inside me. For that I will always be grateful. She inspires me.

"My grandmother was also a very strong individual. There was never a thought that we couldn't be what we wanted to be. We were quite independent, but I understood the importance of family and caring for my community. In our culture, relationships are critical, working together, collaboration, and coming together for a common good. I learned that from my grandmother. I remember getting into the car with my cousins, and my grandmother putting pounds of flour and beans in the backseat, along with all our old clothes so we could drive four hours to Mexicali to share and then go right back home. A couple of weeks later we'd make the trip again.

"Extended family is so important to understanding our culture—and that's how I worked as a teacher—the classroom as a family group. That idea guided me as a professional. I always made sure I knew the families. I didn't wait for a parent conference; I got to know them personally, to know what drove the family dynamic so that I could understand their children better.

"When I first taught it was a team-teaching experience, and it, along with the notion of family, really made a difference. In fact, I asked the principal if we could keep our kids for three years. At that time in the seventies, we had a sixth, seventh, and eighth grade combination. If they were sixth graders we kept them till eighth grade. The difference in their growth compared to the growth in the kids we only had a year was incredible. That's because we got to know the students and got to know each other's teaching strategies. Students saw us as advocates for them. They would do anything for us. They worked hard, and their families supported them. There were families of all income levels, middle class and poor, but they knew that in school they had someone who championed them.

"The culture of any organization, whether a family, school, or district, is an ecosystem, which always does what it can to maintain itself. It's the way things have always been done. When you are brought in to bring about change, it's as if you're changing a tire while the car is moving. You're paying attention to the day-to-day but still looking forward to how you want to get better. When I went to Utah, I didn't make massive change quickly. If I had, it would have been a shock to the system. I respected the existing culture in the Salt Lake district, but the extreme shift in student population demanded that the system adapt. So, I engaged in what I call *re-culturing*. I did not want to imply that the existing system was bad; rather, I wanted to make the culture *itself* one of improvement.

"One of the interesting things about our jobs, but I think you'll find it in any profession, is that even though you move to a new state or city, about 80 percent of your work is the same. The advantage I had when I arrived in Salt Lake City was that I'd already been a successful superintendent in Montebello, California, so my credentials weren't questioned. But once I got to Salt Lake City, I spent 80 percent of my time on the 20 percent of the job, learning the culture. Getting to know people and the community and understanding the culture were very important. My board of education members were extremely welcoming and did everything they could to help me understand the dynamics of

that community and get to know legislators, other superintendents, the state department, and my own staff.

"It was about being very visible and accessible. I had a ninety-
day entry plan. I met key leaders in the community, asking them
what they wanted, what concerned them, and what questions
they had for me. Those three months gave them a chance to get
to know who I was and what I stood for and me the opportunity
to learn about their hopes and dreams for their children and
community.

"At the time I was superintendent, Salt Lake City School District served a population of just over twenty-five thousand students in thirty-eight schools. I was the first woman and the first
person of color to serve as the district's superintendent. There
were barriers. Salt Lake City is the capital city. If anything happens, either statewide or nationally, Salt Lake is usually at the
forefront of it. It is a very progressive city located in a very conser-
vative state. Its population does not mirror that of the rest of the
state. Salt Lake is mostly Democrat; the rest of the state is heavily
Republican. The city is split fifty-fifty in terms of religious affilia-
tion. The rest of the state is predominately Mormon, a community where family is extremely important. They have family
nights on Monday nights, and they rarely have weekend events
because of their religious obligations on Sundays. Saturdays are
spent with kids, and so we worked around those events, understanding that they were always present.

"In some ways that culture mirrors mine. Their religious beliefs guide them. Family is paramount. They are very supportive
of public education. Our board was forward thinking about most
curricular issues. We faced a large influx of minorities with high
poverty rates, which demanded a greater emphasis on ESL and
supplemental lunch programs. We all agreed that these were
necessary.

"However, sometimes I was the only voice speaking out on an issue. People looked to me as a resource and I was always very careful to say I'm not the only resource here, and I'm not the only voice. I don't mind being a strong advocate, but there must be a broader base to move a cause forward. I didn't always want to be viewed as the only one championing it. I believe you do what's right for kids, even though there might be others who disagree with you. I was very fortunate to have a board that was strong in its beliefs about the importance of education and in its commitment to children.

"For instance, my board took a position on no guns on school property in a community that believes strongly in gun rights and ownership, and the law was unclear about not having guns in school. They adopted a resolution that our employees were not allowed to bring guns, even if they had permits, onto our school campuses and into our offices. The rest of the state and legislature were unhappy with the decision, but my board was adamant. Even though its members' belief systems, for the most part, reflected the norms of the community, they were willing to take a stand that differed from the one held by the majority of the people in the area.

"Moving to Salt Lake City required me to move out of my comfort zone. I was born, raised, and worked my way up in the Montebello School District. I relocated to a state where I didn't know a soul and ended up staying there almost eight years. Moving from Montebello to Salt Lake City was the best professional decision of my life. It was great!

"But this career is not for the faint of heart. You just can't be exhausted. It's hard to do. To be a superintendent, you have to really want it. It's time-consuming. It's tough to balance your life. It's a demanding job. Your significant other and your family have to be there with you to support you. Deciding to accept the position in Salt Lake City created a commuter marriage for us. I've been married since 1969 and have one son. They stayed in California where my husband, Frank Robles, continued to work at a major Southern California telecommunications company until he retired.

"Family is extremely important in the Latter-Day Saints (Mormon) faith, and while in Salt Lake City, I lived by myself. I think that was a little uncomfortable for them, the fact that I didn't have my family there with me. They got over it, but the situation was new for them. They did understand that our family was strong and close. I'd go home once a month to visit them. They came to Salt Lake City to see me.

"When you become a superintendent, you are competent, but what you have to always remember is that new circumstances arise. None of us is ever going to have experienced every situation. Being intelligent and competent means that you know when you need additional help, resources, and staff. The word *ego* gets leaders in trouble. My motto: 'I'll only ask you to do what I'm willing to do myself.'

"A close mentor once told me, 'All you have in your position is your integrity. Once that's gone, it doesn't matter what you do.' The straightforward situations are easy; it's the ones that are not black and white that pose the greatest challenge. My litmus test for what I say and do is whether or not I can publicly defend my decisions. If not, I don't go forward with the decision. Others might not like the way I look or talk, but if they can see that I'm consistent and fair and that I'm credible and trustworthy, that's all I can ask for as a leader.

"There was a situation where the secretary was very pleasant to administrators but ignored the custodians and receptionists. They were invisible people to her. It was a reminder for us that all work has dignity and everybody brings his or her value to an organization. We must acknowledge that contribution by saying good morning and hello, by being respectful and treating people as individuals, regardless of title or position. I jokingly say when I have a problem, 'If this is the way I'm being treated as an executive, I can only guess how badly others who don't have any leverage are being treated.'

"My colleagues say I'm real and down-to-earth. My leadership style is easygoing and approachable. People bring me concerns and problems and ways to help the organization. I know my organization, its issues. I keep my ear to the ground and have people I can go to for information. I feel very comfortable asking the custodian or secretary or my assistant superintendents, 'What do you think of this event? How do you feel?' They all view situations differently.

"I always tell young people if you're career bound, make sure you understand that there are going to be challenges. But understand that you have choices and you have options. Women, in particular women of color, who are interested in the superintendency face a dilemma. Women do not support other women. If you are a woman, other women seem to suffer from what I call the 'I could be doing it better' syndrome. In a 1930 article, the author predicted that in the future all the superintendents would be women. In the forties and fifties, there were more women superintendents than there are now. I have heard from many women board members that they would never hire a female superintendent. That attitude probably reflects the stereotypical assumptions that women can't lead complex organizations— they're not tough, they can't make hard decisions—and the idea that women must play certain roles and not others. Yet, everything we know about women's leadership styles, about being collaborative and inclusive, is where more and more businesses are going. I do know men who are great collaborators, but it seems to me that women tend to be natural collaborators more often than men.

"Women leaders, in general, are so involved in doing the work. It's not about the glory, it's not about the attention. It's about the doing. Because they are often watched more closely than men, they must be more mindful than men leaders because any fallout is more critical. They are second-guessed, or just viewed in a different way. If a board wants a reason for not hiring a woman, it will find one. We've got to make it harder for them to find that reason by providing the right experiences for women. We must give women experiences in areas besides curriculum design and instruction. They need to learn about budgets, human resource management, and facilities.

"For males, there's still an old boy network. There's this 'go play golf with me and get to know me,' like a little club. For twenty-five years the American Association of School Administrators hosted a woman's conference. Somebody must've complained recently because the conference is now open to men. Its new title is Women and Emerging Leaders. We asked, 'Who are the emerging leaders? The men? What are the women?' It's the subtle things. If you don't catch them or call people on such moves, they get away with them.

"The typical style of senior leaders in K–12 education is traditionally hierarchical. Power comes from title, position, and background and people use it when it suits them. For example, if you're the superintendent, even if you are doing nothing, you're given power as the superintendent. So too for assistant superintendents and general management. At LACOE, we still have a long way to go in bringing people to a more flat or circular mindset instead of such a hierarchical one. A person with a problem takes it to her supervisor. If the supervisor fails to address the issue, it goes unresolved because the individual won't bypass the hierarchy. That's true in most organizations. Here I'm flattening that structure. People can have such good suggestions, and since they are the ones doing the work, they have suggestions to improve processes and procedures about which I don't have a clue. I don't live it every day. I need that input. I'm willing to break down the barriers, but people have to tell me where they are. We try to communicate and bring stakeholders together around a decision because if you have to implement it, then you should at least be able to have your viewpoint heard on how it's going to be rolled out.

"The best part of coming back home is that I work closely with superintendents. There are eighty superintendents. I already knew quite a few of them, so I got to reconnect with them. It was exciting. The first couple of weeks, I made personal calls to every superintendent. I asked, 'How can we develop a good working relationship between my staff and yours?' We met with them in small groups and established a cabinet-level group to set common goals. I made sure that my staff responded to their needs. For a long time, the superintendents were not connected to this office. They didn't feel that they had an advocate here. Next I developed a ninety-day plan to meet with my board members. I met with every director and anyone from their staff they wanted to include. I asked about what the division did, what its priorities were, what they were working on, what issues they had. I had five questions: What's working? What's not working? If you could change something what would it be? How can my superintendents support your work? and What are the challenges that you're facing financially and otherwise? Because I came in at a time when the state was experiencing budget cuts, I had to quickly talk to the entire employee group. I had small group meetings across the county to discuss the budget crisis. I had to convince them that I'm approachable—not simply this person that stays in her office.

"I am one of a growing number, but today Latina leaders are still not visible in textbooks or in the media, particularly those of us who have been successful. Recently, we honored a Latina scientist, an incredible woman, born in New Mexico. It's not easy to get your hands on information about Latina success stories to share and talk about with young women. I have a granddaughter who is six years old, and I want to share those stories with her. We could do more about putting ourselves out there, saying yes we can make a difference for our second- and third-generation youth, and we can inspire our recent immigrants—telling them, 'Yes, you can make it too.'

"I believe that I have been successful. I earned my Ph.D. in educational policy and administration from the University of Southern California (USC), an M.A. in education from Claremont Graduate School, and a B.A. in history from California State University, Los Angeles (CSULA). I have received numerous awards, including the Association of California School Administrators (ACSA) Kiesel Memorial Distinguished Service Award, the CSULA Distinguished Educator Award, and the USC Association for Advancement of Mexican American Students Award. And I've been involved with a variety of professional organizations—the Council of Great City Schools, Centro de la Familia, and the 2002 Salt Lake City Olympic Education Advisory Committee, to name a few. I am sixty years old. I have been a teacher, a school administrator, a superintendent, and a CEO.

"But my story is not out there, and there are many more success stories not out there for Latinas. It's about humility. It's a matter of time. For years, three of us who are or have been Latina superintendents of large urban districts have been saying we're going to sit down and write a book about Latina leadership. But we get busy. It's something we really need to do because we do have stories to tell."

BIBLIOGRAPHICAL NOTE

The story of Darline Robles came alive through several interviews, the first of which was conducted by Salwa Zaki in March 2006, with follow-up interviews in November 2008 and September 2009. E-mail exchanges from December 2008 through October 2009 further refined the story. Robles's 2006 curriculum vitae, the LACOE website, and the County of Los Angeles Position Description of Superintendent of Schools added depth and understanding. Special thanks to her administrative assistant, Marilyn Musgrave, for facilitating interviews and communication.

nine

A HEALTHY BODY AND A HEALTHY MIND

Beatriz Salcedo-Strumpf

"I WAS BORN IN San Luis Potosí, México, in 1954. I come from a large family—ten children—and I have a twin brother. I am the fifth born. He was the sixth. My siblings have remained close. All of them live in México except for one brother, who lives in Chicago, and he's moving back to México very soon. I lived in México for twenty years until I finished my bachelor's degree at the Universidad de Guadalajara.

"My childhood was fairly typical, except that my relationship with my mother was difficult. She stayed at home and took care of the kids, a chore she complained about because she had studied to be a secretary but was never able to work outside the home. My mother and father often fought about it. As a child I didn't think that she was at all interested in me. I realize now that she was unhappy. I can accept it. For her, it was important to get the chores done every day. Her top priority was keeping the house clean. From an early age, I knew I didn't want to be like her. I wanted a career and money. I resented her for not supporting my schoolwork or my interest in having a career.

"My father was the breadwinner. He didn't spend much time at home because he was always working. He was employed by the Mexican railroad and in the 1950s came to the U.S. to work with the *bracero* program. The bracero program comes from the Spanish word *brazo*, which means arm. It was the result of a series of laws and diplomatic agreements (1947–1964) that allowed the temporary importation of contract laborers from México to the United States. My father spent four or five years in the U.S. right about the time I was born, working in that program. I didn't see him for long periods of time, which was common among Mexicans back then. He went to college through the second year. He loved learning and had a good knowledge of engineering. He also loved animals and passed that love on to me. He was a good father and a wise man.

"We grew up in a middle-class neighborhood and went to public schools. We took a bus every day. We attended the Catholic church, of course. We celebrated Christmas but usually not anyone's birthday. In fact, my mother totally forgot my fifteenth birthday. I have beautiful memories of Christmas at home. It was always a large celebration with the extended family. Those were happy times.

"Three of my grandparents were from México. My grandfather on my father's side was from Valencia, Spain. I only briefly met my father's side of the family. I was very young and my grandfather was very old when he came to live with us. A short time later, he died at our home.

"It was my grandmother on my mother's side who inspired me and was my role model. She was optimistic and extremely healthy—a most wonderful woman. Her husband, my grandfather, was an alcoholic. He died before I was born. She worked hard to provide food and housing for her family. She washed clothes for people and bought clothes from a local factory and then sold them to poor people on installments. One summer I lived with her. I was her favorite granddaughter. We had a special relationship. At the time I went to the U.S., she didn't know how to read or write. I would write to her and she had to have someone else read my letters and write back to me. She learned to read and write just so she could correspond with me. I was very proud of her. I learned a great deal from her.

"When I started college I decided to train as an aerobics instructor, but I've always been interested in languages. So, in my second year I went to France for three months to study the language. I'd already started to take English classes by then—night classes for three years—and each afternoon I studied Italian and French. In my junior year I was given an assistantship in a small college in the U.S. to study English. At the gym where I worked, everyone saw me as efficient, friendly, and trustworthy, and that's why one of the women clients helped me get the assistantship through a Presbyterian church even though I was Catholic. I ended up in Ohio of all places for two full years at the College of Wooster. The assistantship was especially designed for me. I worked as a teaching assistant in beginning Spanish classes helping the professors grade students and develop cultural activities for their classes. It was a great experience and it brought me to the States.

"Four of my brothers and sisters also went to the university. One is now a dentist, one an engineer, one an architect, and one a psychologist. The other five of us finished high school. I'm the only one to enroll in a doctoral degree program. I am currently reworking my dissertation and hope to finish shortly. I get along very well with my brothers and sisters, especially with my sister Marta. She has had a great deal of tragedy in her life. She became a single mother when she was eighteen. My family ostracized her; she attempted suicide and ended up delivering a sick baby who died when he was six months old. A couple of years later she had another son, who, at the age of twelve, was killed by a car while crossing the street. My oldest son was very close in age to him. I think her tragedies have brought us closer. We speak on the phone once a week. My twin brother is already a grandfather. My mother used to call him 'the smart one.' For me, that turned out to be quite ironic because he never went to college and I am still engaged in formal education and the pursuit of knowledge.

"From the time I was little I knew I would marry a foreigner. I dated men from France, Italy, Germany, and Ecuador. I met quite a few Americans through the medical school in Guadalajara because I wanted to practice my English.

"There is *machismo* everywhere in the world—just different degrees of it. The difference between Mexican and American men is that the American men I met were reliable. The Mexican men I dated were never punctual and often undependable. When an American said he would call me at 5 p.m., that's when the phone rang. I liked that. It was important to me. The Mexican men I dated never seemed to be on time, and sometimes they got drunk and completely forgot our date. By the time I was in my twenties, I was tired of the machismo in our Mexican society. I didn't necessarily set out to marry an American, but that's one of the reasons I did.

"The most attractive thing about my husband, Kenneth Strumpf, is that he treats me well. He is polite. He is always punctual. He perseveres in our relationship. Marriage takes work! I'm not saying that some Latin men aren't like this as well, but I found it first in Kenneth. In México we live in a world that is still primarily patriarchal, and some men don't understand how to deal with women, especially women with careers. In fact, most men in the world are patriarchal and *machistas*, but my husband isn't, and if he ever is I can call him on it and he changes. I tried this with a couple of Mexican boyfriends—well, forget it. I'm sure there are Mexican men who are understanding, just as there are violent American men, but I never came across any.

"Kenneth and I married in 1982. We dated for two years prior to that. I don't think we ever thought of living in México, even though Kenneth was living in México when we met. He studied medicine there. He eventually transferred to New York University in New York City. At about the same time he transferred I was awarded an assistantship at Marquette University in Wisconsin so that I could enroll in a master's degree program. We only saw each other every six months or so. It was a long-distance relationship that happened to work. After two years he was able to do his residency in Milwaukee so we were together again. We stayed there for five years before going to Connecticut and finally ending up in Fayetteville in upstate New York.

"We had our first child two years after we got married and then the second one five years later. Our oldest son, Daniel, is twenty-four and a journalist for The Associated Press. He lives in New York City. Our son David is a sophomore at Syracuse University. He wants to be a Marine. They are very different boys. Daniel is smart and studious. He's a great kid and we get along quite well. He's not very happy in journalism because of the way the technology is changing the field. He's thinking about going to law school or working for the government. He'd like to live abroad. David is also great. He's a very funny man, very different from Daniel. He enjoys life. He's athletic. He does well in school. Now that both boys are out of the house, it's just me, my husband, and the cats.

"I take care of twenty-two cats! It's much more than a hobby. I spay and neuter them and put them up for adoption. I write a blog, which entails more work than you might imagine. The primary purpose of the blog is to help get these cats adopted, to get them good homes. I do it on my own, with my own money.

"I am very energetic. Once I open my eyes in the morning, it's nonstop for me. I get up early, usually by 5:30, and feed the cats. I have a cup of coffee and either run six miles or lift weights for an hour. I've been a runner for thirty-five years. I carry my sneakers with me every time I travel. Running gives me energy and stamina. It makes my brain work better and keeps me healthy and optimistic. Exercising is more important than eating for me. It's like breathing.

"I leave for work at the State University of New York [SUNY] in Oswego at around seven. It's an hour's drive. I immediately teach three classes in a row. In the afternoon I teach another class, grade papers, and organize cultural activities for the students. I'm home for dinner and 'husband time.' I prepare for the next day and read or write until late each evening. My day usually ends around eleven.

"I am happiest when I am writing well, when I'm giving voice to the oppressed and disenfranchised in this world. For example, I recently wrote a short story about non-English-speaking immigrants to this country. Sometimes I write about animals. One story features a cat that talks and tells us about how horrible it is to be declawed. So, I give voice to people and animals who can't speak for themselves.

"I write in Spanish and English. Because I came from México and English is not my first language, I've had to work hard to find my own voice. The first draft of anything I write is always in Spanish because I feel more comfortable writing literature in my native language. I used to have someone translate for me, but I'm more confident now doing it myself. When it's an important literary work I seek the advice of my editor to make sure my translations are accurate. In poetry especially it's crucial to have the translation precise or you ruin the meaning. I recently authored a novel, *E-Mail for Lovers*, which was initially published in Spanish and then in English. I wrote a compilation of short stories, four of which have appeared in prestigious literary magazines here in the U.S., *Revista Literaria Baqiana* in Miami, for example, and *Revista de Curiosidad Cultural Destiempos* in México A number of my poems have been published in both countries. I think my English skills are adequate, but if I don't know a word I either ask my husband or go to the dictionary. My blog is bilingual because it forces me to practice writing correctly.

"The biggest turning point in my career was getting the teaching job at SUNY Oswego. (Beatriz is an assistant professor.) I love teaching even though it's very time-consuming and draining to do it right. When I teach Spanish Literature 101, I do it in Spanish but often explain things in English so that students who don't speak Spanish fluently can understand and get the meaning or significance of the pieces of work we examine in the class. I teach all levels of students from freshmen to seniors, from beginners in Spanish 101 to advanced in Spanish 302. I use theater, music, technology, and the laboratory (repetition) to support my students' learning. I also mentor them by addressing their concerns about cultural issues, such as discrimination and bias. As a teacher I reach out to my students, to help them eliminate stereotypes at all levels, to ensure that everyone can understand everyone else.

"I also host a radio show each Saturday, which runs from five to six in the evening. It's called *Accentuated Words* and is all in Spanish. It features taped and live interviews, book reviews, local news, and rarely heard Spanish music. The show involves a tremendous amount of research on my part.

"Currently, I've been relearning French for the fun of it and studying lines for a play, *Mujeres de Arena* (Women of Sand). The play features the testimonials of women who have been murdered or are missing in Ciudad Juárez, México. Over 575 women have been murdered since 1993, and more than 600 are missing. Most worked in *maquilas* or sweatshops, many of them migrants. Acting in this play is a way for me to let people know what is happening, to make people aware. Just because these women are poor, people think they do not matter. I want others to know what the reality truly is.

"I always think in the present—that this could be the last day of my life. I try and live that way, enjoying each minute of every day. I persevere in all aspects of my work. When I start something, I keep to it. I keep reading, keep writing, keep running, and keep strong. I never forget my roots.

"Being married to an American has helped me to assimilate more successfully into mainstream U.S. life. My husband is Jewish so I've come to learn a great deal about that culture as well. I find culture interesting. To this day I'm not fully assimilated into the American culture. Having two cultures gives me a unique perspective and two distinct ways of dealing with people. I function well in both the U.S. and México.

"I'm aware of the stereotypes that exist about nonnative English speakers. I've never experienced discrimination because I don't speak perfect English. Most people just say I have a cute accent. The only time I ever felt discriminated against was in Milwaukee. Everyone there was blond and then here I come. They thought I was a Native American and treated me very differently. That was a real surprise to me. I was teaching Italian at a local high school. One day, I heard a few students whispering, 'Don't pay attention to her, she's an Indian.' That was a first for me. I was shocked. I'd never encountered discrimination before in my life. I told them I would kick them out of class if they kept talking, and they stopped. They were basically good kids.

"I believe I am successful. In the United States success is defined to a large extent in terms of how much money you make. I define success as being happy with yourself and with your career and having balance in your life. Together they create a healthy mind. You have to be physically healthy too. All three—happiness, balance, and health—are related. If you are healthy you stand a far better chance of being happy and if you are happy you have peace of mind. If I am truly happy, I am passionate about what I do and I earn credibility. If I have credibility and passion, I believe that money and success will come. I am fair and honest, and I demonstrate my integrity to others by doing what I say I'm going to do. I am compassionate. Compassion keeps me accessible. I might not get rich, but I will make enough money so I don't have to worry. If I have integrity, compassion, and passion I believe that I will have a comfortable life. A healthy mind, a healthy body, and balance in life: That is success for me."

BIBLIOGRAPHICAL NOTE

The story of Beatriz Salcedo-Strumpf evolved from a series of interviews, e-mail exchanges, and an examination of her website at www.palabrasacentuadas.wordpress.com, her blog at www .beatrizsalcedostrumpf.wordpress.com, and her curriculum vitae.

ten

AQUÍ NO HAY VIOLETAS DISMINUÍDAS

W HEN WE SAY someone is no shrinking violet, we mean that the person is very self-confident and thrives under a variety of conditions. A bold not a timid woman—an apt descriptor for Sarita Brown, Tina Cordova, Sally Garza Fernandez, Carmella Franco, Christine Johnson, Thelma López-Lira, Darline Robles, and Beatriz Salcedo-Strumpf.

Each of these eight women encountered situations that others might seek to avoid. López-Lira and Salcedo-Strumpf moved from México, and Robles spent years in a commuter marriage—bold steps that took courage. These Latinas are tough. Franco explains the way she faces recalcitrant boards as "not gore" but "strategy." Johnson was fired from a job she loved. Fernandez tackled corporate America and left a blossoming career to embrace the unknowns of business ownership and entrepreneurship. Cordova shifted career goals from becoming a doctor to becoming a roofing contractor and never looked back. Each faced personal adversity—illness, family loss, divorce—that had an impact on her professional career. They did not shrink away but faced their challenges head-on.

These women are independent and strong, and they stand up for what they believe is right. López-Lira and Johnson in particular refer to themselves as independent and strong. Those characteristics seem embedded deep within all these stories. In fact, Franco suggests, "What doesn't knock you out will make you a better fighter." Their strength manifests itself in their sense of honor and an all-encompassing need for credibility. Fernandez calls it crucial. López-Lira must be able to do what she says she will do and do it with integrity because it makes her credible. Robles's "litmus test for what [she] say[s] and do[es] is whether or not [she] can publicly defend [her] decisions." She simply does not engage in activities that impinge on her standing as a person worthy of trust. Franco anticipates political oversight and thinks about every angle of a decision. Johnson perhaps summed it up best when she said, "I've taken numerous risks professionally, stood on principle, and spoken out when others would not," and "I live my life with integrity and gusto."

These women are hardworking, focused problem solvers with can-do spirits. In her stint in corporate America, Fernandez was consistently hired to solve problems, whether they had to do with environmental hazards or flagging product markets. In fact, she says her passion is to solve problems, to build, and to succeed. Robles says, "My leadership style is easygoing and approachable," and "I'm not going to settle for less than the best." She and the others don't ask those around them to do anything they wouldn't do. Even López-Lira, the only one of the eight who cannot delegate some of her responsibilities, works as hard or harder than the individuals she employs or works with in her practice. These women seem ready to face any test set before them. Johnson claims her very nature derives from the can-do spirit of the West in which many of these women grew up.

Along the same lines, they are action oriented, forward thinking, and success driven. Brown concentrates on the ideal and then works to make it happen. Franco went to work in a new school district one day after retiring from another. Fernandez, already the head of five firms in Arizona, went into partnership with her daughter to operate a Chicago-based salon and spa because the opportunity was there for the taking. These women take action, but they also plan and reflect on what they are about to do. Robles and Franco went into their districts with ninety-day plans. And Franco cautions, "You have to know how to shape your battles." Fernandez says that "you must continually reflect on what you are doing and what is going on around you so that you can move your vision beyond what it is today." They all devise ways to measure progress, whether they run education-related organizations or businesses, teach, or practice medicine.

They want to succeed. Fernandez describes herself as an "extreme overachiever. More determined, more focused, more disciplined. I have made sacrifices, but I have also gained great rewards. I work very hard to ensure my success." Similarly, Cordova remarks, "I worked hard, I learned, I persevered, and I succeeded." And Brown notes, "I was tested and found I could depend on myself. I knew I could produce and that I could work hard and succeed." They all come back to the fact that success takes hard work—a lot of it.

In their quest for success, they work through people, not against them. They engage and enable people. When Fernandez moves into a new situation, she becomes a sponge focusing on perceptions and subtleties. They learn the culture of those they interact with and use well-honed interpersonal skills to move their organizations forward. Although Robles and Cordova speak Spanish, they work with a unique group of Spanish speakers—immigrants—whose backgrounds differ from their own. And while López-Lira emigrated from México she works primarily with Anglos raised in Texas. López-Lira explains the way she approaches these cultural differences: "I am tolerant. . . . I don't try to change people who don't want to change," and "I accept people the way they are." Similarly, Johnson notes, "I love people and intuitively know when they are with me or not. I have great empathy for others and that makes me more responsive to them." She worked through people at Denver Community College to shape a more tolerant, receptive culture. At the Woodland Joint Unified School District Franco faced a culture that promoted accepting the way things were in a low-achieving school. She patiently removed peripheral obstacles until the root of the problem stood out and could be tackled. For Robles, Utah represented the challenge of *re-culturing*. She says, "The culture of any organization, whether a family, school, or district, is an ecosystem, which always does what it can to maintain itself. When you are brought in to bring about change, it's as if you're changing a tire while the car is moving." Brown needs to get past the "lethal comfort level" when it comes to the achievement gap. "Somehow we feel that just by talking about it something has happened." For her, talking about it is "like setting the table for dinner." She asks: "But, where is the food?"

These Latinas are passionate about what they do and love doing it. They persevere. "I love the word *passionate*," says Robles. "It speaks to the core of any leader's role." She and Johnson agree that passion distinguishes people who are average from people who are excellent, the doers from the keepers of the status quo, because it signals that you care. And Fernandez notes that "people get excited because of the passion effective leaders demonstrate." These women love what they do. "I rarely just 'do' a job," Brown says. "I engage in a passion," and "I see what I do as my life's calling." Brown's sentiment is emphasized time and again across these stories. López-Lira loves her job. Franco admits that she couldn't do her job without "absolutely loving it" and knowing that she's making a difference.

And they do so with energy and enthusiasm and no thought of slowing down.

They are optimistic, happy people. Johnson says she's "been blessed with good health, optimism, energy, and joy in living." They stay physically and mentally fit. Salcedo-Strumpf equates exercising to breathing. It's that important. And she, like the others, continually challenges herself mentally. She worked on her doctorate degree, she learns French. Cordova fishes because it makes her relax and reflect. If López-Lira starts "losing energy [she] give[s] [her]self a few minutes of fantasizing about how good [her] last vacation was and how great [her] next one will be. Doing so allows [her] to recharge." They all strive for balance in their lives. Fernandez quit corporate America because she felt that she didn't know her daughter. She stresses, "It is important to not take yourself too seriously, to have balance in your life. The world is not all about you. You need to look around and ask yourself: What have I done today for others that is good?"

They are pragmatic. They recognize that gender and ethnic bias exist. Robles asserts that women leaders "are often watched more closely than men, they must be more mindful than men leaders because any fallout is more critical." Cordova sees it as a matter of competency. "A woman must be incredibly competent at what she does." And "wise," says Franco. Brown states bluntly, "The 'landscape' is biased against Latina women. . . . I am constantly tested. . . . In some respects the situation is analogous to 'It's cold outside, so put a coat on.'" In other words, deal with it.

These women have intestinal fortitude. They deal with it. For some, dealing with bias and discrimination demands they take an extra step. Salcedo-Strumpf prepares for a role in the play *Juárez* because it's a way for her to let people know what is happening to women in that city. Franco clearly takes a proactive stance. She deems it crucial "to help others [Latinas in particular], learn how to avoid the pitfalls, to keep their integrity intact, to get through situations as unscathed as they can, and to be better people for it"—and "to open doors for them." Robles expands on its importance. "I am one of a growing number, but today Latina leaders are still not visible in textbooks or in the media, particularly those of us who have been successful. [Our] stor[ies] [are] not out there and we have stories to tell."

Johnson puts it rather eloquently: "One of our greatest gifts is time and the use of time, so I've been disciplined about making my time count—using it well, using it to do good, using it to be a person worth emulating." These women are indeed worth emulating. Their stories have taught us much. They've left us with words they live by:

⬥ Follow your passion.
⬥ Be true to yourself and faithful to your word.
⬥ Measure your decisions against public disclosure.
⬥ Take care of yourself, your body and your mind.
⬥ Focus on your goals and don't be afraid to strive for success.
⬥ Use your skills to build and shape your organization and its people.
⬥ Work with people's cultures, not against them.
⬥ Know that Latina discrimination exists. Be well prepared for it.
⬥ Be a role model or mentor to other Latinas.

Aquí No Hay Violetas Disminuídas

These are not the words of shrinking violets. There are no shrinking violets here.

DEFINITIONS

http://en.wiktionary.org/wiki/shrinking_violet
http://www.plkcastar.edu.hk/english/fun2_idioms.html

eleven

PROJECT METHODOLOGY

THE STORIES PRESENTED in this volume are part of an ongoing qualitative research project conducted by a team of
women academics from a variety of disciplines including business, education, sports, public administration, and hospitality.
We recognized, as various sources have documented, that despite
the progress of women in the general workforce, women continue to be underrepresented in each of our fields of study. Much
of the literature about and research on leadership has been
written by and about men, primarily White men. In addition,
leadership has traditionally been examined using male behaviors
and characteristics as the norm against which women are as-
sessed. The leadership literature presents mixed messages about
whether women leaders function differently than men who hold
comparable leadership positions. We took the position that the
issue is really effectiveness rather than gender. And that effective
leaders, male or female, subscribe to similar beliefs about leadership and act more similarly than differently when they enact
those roles.

Our extensive investigation of the leadership literature in our
fields found the body of knowledge on leadership to be dis-
jointed, with some researchers investigating a particular approach to leadership (e.g., transformational leadership) and

others examining a completely different, but equally important, aspect crucial to effective leadership (e.g., cognitive framing). Based on our assumption that effective leadership is not gender specific, we synthesized existing literature into a series of nine tenets of effective leadership (see Table 11.1). This synthesis created a basic structure that captures what we believe to contribute to effective leadership.

We purposefully selected participants for their ability to inform the study (Lincoln & Guba, 1985; Merriam, 1998; Yin, 2003).

TABLE 11.1
Nine Tenets of Effective Leadership

Nine Tenets of Effective Leadership
Effective leaders are passionate about their organizations. They exhibit extraordinary commitment not only to the organization but to its people.
Effective leaders are reflective. They are self-aware, self-disciplined, self-confident, and self-assured.
Effective leaders are competent. They possess the intelligence and mental capacity to get the job done.
Effective leaders are great communicators. They have their finger on the pulse of the organization.
Effective leaders understand the role that culture plays in shaping the way they lead.
Effective leaders possess the physical and emotional stamina, energy, and resilience needed to persevere in the long run.
Effective leaders are focused yet forward thinking.
Effective leaders respect and value individuality.
Effective leaders possess credibility. The building blocks of credibility are trust, integrity, and power.

These women were viewed as effective leaders using two general estimates of effectiveness: reputation among peers and longevity of experience. In addition, we strove for ethnic, geographic, and institutional diversity within each field. For the first books in this series, the women chosen also had control over organizational budgets and more than five employees who report directly to them. In this book, we expanded the definition of leadership to include women who are leaders in their fields but who do not necessarily directly supervise employees, a move that allowed us to include a medical doctor and an author.

Because leadership is affected by context, it is difficult to study a leader independent of context. Therefore, qualitative case study was chosen as an appropriate methodology for the project (Yin, 2003). Case study design enabled the researchers to compare the leaders across organizational types, looking for common threads and patterns in their responses (Babbie, 2001; Miles & Huberman, 1994; Yin, 2003). A semistructured interview protocol was developed and piloted prior to participant interviews (Lincoln & Guba, 1985; Miles & Huberman, 1994; Yin, 2003). Interviews were conducted using a combination of face-to-face, telephone, and e-mail exchanges and took two to four hours to complete. All verbal exchanges were tape-recorded and transcribed. Data were systematically categorized by themes and patterns of responses delineated by multiple researchers to ensure consistency and validity. Additional information pertaining to the leader and her organization was gathered for the case studies via college documents, résumés and curricula vitae, newspaper articles, and the Internet. Once the cases were written, they were reviewed by the research team, and each case was shared with its respective participant for accuracy and trustworthiness.

Although other reports of this research focus on the leaders' experiences in relationship to the tenets of effective leadership, the work presented in the "Journeys to Leadership Series" introduces their individual and unique voices as they discuss their values and the events that have shaped them as leaders in their respective fields.

REFERENCES

Babbie, E. (2001). *The practice of social research* (9th ed.). Belmont, CA: Wadsworth/Thomson Learning.

Lincoln, Y. S., & Guba, E. G. (1985). *Naturalistic inquiry.* Newbury Park, CA: Sage.

Merriam, S. B. (1998). *Qualitative research and case study applications in education.* San Francisco: Jossey-Bass.

Miles, M. B., & Huberman, A. M. (1994). *Qualitative data analysis* (2nd ed.). Thousand Oaks, CA: Sage.

Yin, R. K. (2003). *Case study research: Design and methods.* Thousand Oaks, CA: Sage.

INDEX

Abrams, Stan, 42
abuse of power, Franco on, 58–59
Accelerating LAtino Student Success
   (ALASS), 19
Access and Success Project, 73
achievement gap
   Brown on, 12
   Franco on, 56–58
ACSA. *See* Association of California
   School Administrators
ADHD. *See* attention deficit hyperac-
   tivity disorder
Aguilerra, Elizabeth, 82
ALASS. *See* Accelerating LAtino Stu-
   dent Success
Alexander, Lamar, 68, 76
Anheuser-Busch, 39
Aniko Salon and Spa, 43
Aragon, Art, 49
Association of California School Ad-
   ministrators (ACSA), Superin-
   tendents Academy, 53
attention deficit hyperactivity disorder
   (ADHD), 88

biculturalism
   Johnson on, 66–67

Latina leaders and, 4–6
   Robles on, 99
   Salcedo-Strumpf on, 118
   See also culture
Biden, Jill, 16
bilingualism. *See* language
boundaries, López-Lira on, 93
boxing, Franco on, 49–50, 53
Boyer, Ernest, 79–80
bracero program, 112
Brown, Sarita, 10*f*, 11–22
Busch, August III, 42

California Association of Bilingual
   Education (CABE), 51
calling
   Brown on, 12–13
   Johnson on, 75
cancer
   Cordova on, 31
   Fernandez on, 44
   Franco on, 61
caring. *See* passion
case management teams, educational,
   73
Catholicism
   Cordova on, 26, 33

Index

Index

Cordova on, 27–29
Fernandez on, 38, 43
Franco on, 59
Latina leaders and, 5, 125–126
López-Lira on, 90
Robles on, 98, 106
Salcedo-Strumpf on, 118–119
diversity, Latina leaders and, 6

education
Brown on, 11–22
Cordova on, 27–29
Fernandez on, 38, 42, 45
Franco on, 49–63
Johnson on, 65–82
Latina leaders and, 3
López-Lira on, 87–88
Robles on, 97–109
Salcedo-Strumpf on, 111–119
Education Commission of the States,
69
Emily Griffith Opportunity School,
70
energy
Brown on, 12
Johnson on, 74–75
Latina leaders and, 125
Salcedo-Strumpf on, 116
See also stamina
ethics. See values
ethnic identity
Brown on, 13–14
Cordova on, 27
Franco on, 51
Latina leaders and, 6
Robles on, 99

Excelencia in Education, 11, 17–19
Explorers program, 38

faith. See religion
family
Brown on, 13–14, 16, 19–21
Cordova on, 25–27, 32–33
Fernandez on, 35–37, 43–44
Franco on, 49–51, 60–61
Johnson on, 65–68
Latina leaders and, 2–3
López-Lira on, 85, 87, 93
Robles on, 99–100, 103–104
Salcedo-Strumpf on, 111–116
See also work-life balance
fathers
Brown on, 13, 20–21
Cordova on, 26–27
Johnson on, 67
Latina leaders and, 2–3
Salcedo-Strumpf on, 112
Fernandez, Sally Garza, 34f, 35–46
Fernandez Enterprises, 35
Flores, Aurelia, 8
focus, Fernandez on, 41–42
Fox, Vicente, 76
Franco, Carmella, 48f, 49–63

General Motors, 38–39
Goodman, Emma, 97
graduation rates, for Latino students,
19
grandmothers
Franco on, 50
Latina leaders and, 2–3

~ 135 ~

Also available from Stylus

Journeys to Leadership Series

The *Journeys to Leadership* Series presents the lives and motivations of successful women who have reached the pinnacle of their careers. It features stories about extraordinary women who have found paths to success—whether by leading a college or university, by becoming successful scholars in science and engineering, or by thriving in some other male-dominated arena.

Answering the Call
African American Women in Higher Education Leadership
Beverly L. Bower and Mimi Wolverton

This book presents the stories, and the reflections on their paths to leadership, of seven African American women. Five are, or have been, college presidents; three have devoted a good portion of their lives to leadership in higher education policy at state and/or national levels.

Each has been the first woman, or first African American, or first African American woman in one or more of the positions of authority that she has held.

Along the way, they have overcome the double bind of sexism and racism that can inhibit the professional attainment of African American women, particularly as they move toward the top of their professions.

At a time when national demographic data indicate that a significant turnover in college leadership is about to occur—presenting increased opportunities for women and minorities—these African American women leaders hope that the strategies they describe, the insights they impart, the experiences they recount, and, most of all, the passion they have sustained for the betterment of and greater inclusiveness in higher education, will inspire the next generation of women to answer the leadership call.

Women at the Top
What Women University and College Presidents Say About Effective Leadership
Mimi Wolverton, Beverly L. Bower and Adrienne E. Hyle

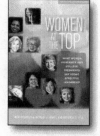

"A book that is a truly exceptional contribution to the literature on leadership. The authors' distillation of the interviews to derive the nine tenets of effective leadership make this a must read for aspiring leaders and followers in higher education. I especially liked the fact that the tenets were tucked away in the back after the authors' thoughtful discussion of the obstacles of this 'road less traveled.' They highlight the speed bumps and crossroads that traditionally hold women and people of color from leadership positions.

"*Women at the Top* is inspirational because most women who read it will see themselves trying to balance their competing family priorities with career paths and can say, 'I can do this too.' The future looks bright indeed for women who aspire to leadership roles in higher education, and this deeply personal and reflective book will serve as a guidebook and resource for other women who seek leadership roles in the nation's colleges and universities."—*Teachers College Record*

22883 Quicksilver Drive
Sterling, VA 20166-2102

Subscribe to our e-mail alerts: www.Styluspub.com